Tackle Windsurfing

Glenn Taylor

Tackle Windsurfing

Adapted by Graham Fuller

Stanley Paul
London Melbourne Sydney Auckland Johannesburg

Stanley Paul & Co. Ltd

An imprint of Hutchinson Publishing Group

17–21 Conway Street, London W1P 6JD

Hutchinson Group (Australia) Pty Ltd
30–32 Cremorne Street, Richmond South, Victoria 3121
PO Box 151, Broadway, New South Wales 2007

Hutchinson Group (NZ) Ltd
32–34 View Road, PO Box 40–086, Glenfield, Auckland 10

Hutchinson Group (SA) (Pty) Ltd
PO Box 337, Bergvlei 2012, South Africa

First published in Great Britain 1982

© Glenn Taylor 1979 and 1982

Filmset by Willmer Brothers Limited
Birkenhead, Merseyside

Printed in Great Britain by The Anchor Press Ltd
and bound by Wm Brendon & Son Ltd,
both of Tiptree, Essex

British Library Cataloguing in Publication Data

Taylor, Glenn
  Tackle windsurfing.
  1. Windsurfing
  I. Title   II. Fuller, Graham
  797.1′24   GV811.63.W56

ISBN 0 09 145041 1

Photographs are reproduced by courtesy of:
Christopher Mullin, J. E. S., Windsurfing
International Inc., Mary Pinkney, Ken Such,
Tara Schweitzer, George Ham, Charles
Carrenza, Fred Ostermann GmbH & Co., Lee
Dobbs (Corpus Christi *Times*), Verna West,
Waterfun Inc., Stamford, Connecticut, the
Accelerator Co. and the author.

Contents

Acknowledgements

My thanks to all the individuals whose photographs, ideas, and assistance made this book possible.

Special thanks to Christopher Mullin whose 'how-to' photos enabled the project to begin, and to Christine Newman whose critiques and advice were invaluable in guiding my writing, and who acted very skilfully in the role of model for many of the photographs that demonstrate basic windsurfing techniques. Windsurfing is used through-out this book as a description of the activity pioneered by the makers of the original Windsurfer board and full acknowledgement goes to them for their early and continuing inspirational work.

Thanks also to Lucille Taylor, my mother, without whose support I would not have had the opportunity to write the book.

Many thanks to Bep Thijs, Dago Benz, Per S. Fjaestad and, of course, Jim Drake and Hoyle and Diane Schweitzer, without whom there would be no subject for this book.

Finally, thanks to San Francisco Bay, whose windy challenge helped many of us begin to realize the potential of the windsurfer sailboard.

Glenn Taylor

Chapter One
Introduction

A new water sport has taken Europe by storm and the excitement here has already been echoed in every corner of the world. What is this new sport? It is the use of a 'free-sail system', and it is popularly called 'windsurfing' after the registered trade name Windsurfer.

The idea of windsurfing originated during 1966 and 1967, after conversations between Hoyle Schweitzer, a vice president of a computer software company, and James Drake, an aircraft designer, at one of Schweitzer's frequent parties at his Californian home. The two men wanted to overcome the problems associated with their different hobbies. Drake's problems concerned the difficulties and time involved in rigging and launching a sailing boat, and Schweitzer's the restricted areas and times when conditions were right for surfing. Drake mentioned to Schweitzer that for the last five years he had been toying with a plan to develop a sailing surfboard, and Schweitzer was intrigued. Thus windsurfing was born. Ten years later, the sport had ecstatic adherents in France, Germany, Russia, Brazil, Australia, Holland, Sweden, Israel, Kenya, Japan – and many other countries. Between 1973 and 1977, more than 100,000 free-sail systems were put into use, and the number increases substantially each year.

Figure 1: *A city worker with a lake or the sea near by can use a windsurfing sailboard for after-work relaxation. It can be launched nearly anywhere, and assembly time is only a few minutes*

What is the attraction? What creates the excitement? What do you feel when you sail a windsurfing sailboard? The first thing is the speed – sailboards are fast, and moreover, the *feeling* of speed is strong. The nearby water blurs as you sweep over it. The faster you go, the more the nose of the board lifts from the water and the more widely the spray from the bow is shot to the sides. In high winds the board takes off in great leaps from the wave tops and becomes totally airborne, giving the sensational thrill of flying through space in free fall.

The craft's manoeuvrability adds yet more charm to the sensations. With perhaps a hundred hours of practice, a sailor can become so used to his craft that it is like an extension of himself. It can be made to stop, go backwards, sideways, or perform any combination of these manoeuvres, in an instant. In a strong wind windsurfing becomes strenuous, but the thrill is greater because the speed of the board increases with the wind speed. To get that added ounce of pull to achieve even more speed, you find yourself exerting just a bit more effort to contract straining muscles still further – and the reward is instantaneous: the board goes faster. When every ounce of energy has been expended, you come in tired but exhilarated, and you know that this exercise has increased both your windsurfing skill and your strength. As your strength and skill increase, so does the time you can spend on the water. Next week you will be able to achieve perhaps another quarter of an hour's exciting sailing before you tire. Fatigued

Figure 2: *When a windsurfing sailor falls from the craft, the sail folds down to the water leaving the board level on the surface with little of its shape projecting into the wind*

as you may be at the moment you return to the beach, you will look forward eagerly to your next adventure on your board.

The range of conditions in which a windsurfing sailboard can be used varies widely. It can be successfully operated by a beginner with a few hours of practice – though perhaps only in light winds on calm water – while in the hands of an expert the tiny sailboard can be driven through mountainous waves in winds that make most other small pleasure boaters seek shelter. Even so, wind-surfing has an absolutely unexpected safety record – as of 1981 the known toll of fatalities directly due to the craft is far fewer than those of driving automobiles per passenger mile (at least thirty times fewer). The sport is probably over 1000 times safer (per participant hour)

than downhill snow skiing or bicycle riding.

This may be the safest of all modern sports, far safer than surfing, water skiing, snow skiing, conventional sailing – even than bicycling. It seems almost unnatural that this safety record should exist, considering the thrills one can get from the sport, but the windsurfing board *is* extremely safe. 'Won't the sail or mast land on your head?' the spectator inquires. Yes, it can; but to do so it has to fall *upwind*, and it can do that only very slowly and with a relatively weak impact. 'What if *you* fall on the board or mast?' This is far less serious than falling from a bicycle, since the Windsurfer board is soft, resilient polyethylene plastic cushioned by foam filling inside, and both board and mast rest atop an even more yielding surface – water.

Furthermore, windsurfing is easy. Just about anyone who attends a Certified Windsurfing School can be taught how to sail. At a good school, over 90 per cent of all beginners learn in four to six hours. True, self-taught students of windsurfing take about three times longer to get the

Figure 3: *When a sailing boat capsizes, quite a bit of its bulk is left up in the wind, allowing it to drift rather quickly. Until the craft is completely upright again, the sailor must usually remain in the water*

hang of it, but even they will succeed, and with little risk, if they just keep at it for a few days.

Besides the pleasure that the sensations of windsurfing provide, and besides its offer of mental escape, what else is the sport good for? Simply stated, windsurfing is great *recreation*. This is highly entertaining exercise. More fun than lifting weights or doing press-ups, windsurfing is almost as good for your muscles and even better for your coordination. And you don't have to be in tip-top physical condition to begin the sport. It is only your endurance that will be limited by your physical condition. Typically, novices can sail windsurfing sailboards for one to two hours in moderate winds (to force 3, or 10 knots). After one month of practice twice weekly, they can double that time – and

after three months just about triple it. The physical demands are very similar to those of snow skiing. If you really like the sensations of windsurfing and want to stay out and sail as long as possible at every available opportunity, there are aids called 'harnesses' (described in Chapter 12) which permit good boardsailors to sail every daylight hour, continuously, in winds of up to force 5 (20 knots).*

What does it cost? Relative to other popular sports which use special equipment, very little. Initially the output of capital required to purchase a sailboard appears high to some people, but once you own one additional expenses are low. If you are a moderate user of your sailboard and only sail three hours a week for six months, the sport will cost you less than 50p an

---

*Wind speeds will generally be given in this book in Beaufort Scale numbers (or 'force' numbers) rather than in knots. Appendix 1 lists the miles-per-hour wind speeds associated with the Beaufort numbers 0 to 10. Also, the metric system will be used throughout, but Imperial conversions will be given in many instances.

Figure 4: *What do you do when you get tired? As long as the sail is left down in the water, the board will provide a stable place to rest*

Figure 5 (opposite): *At slightly over 18 kilograms (40 pounds), the board is easily lifted even by a small sailor*

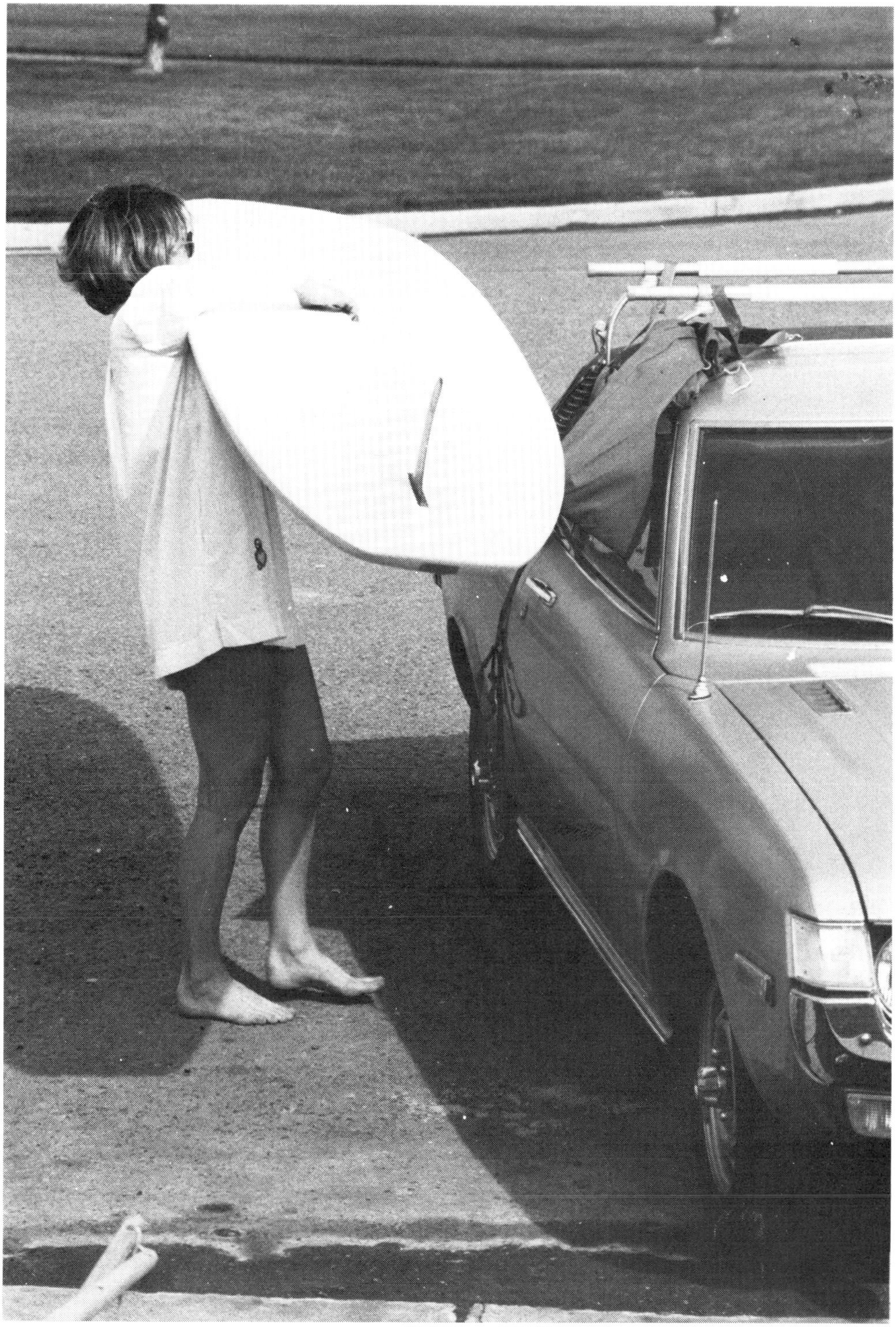

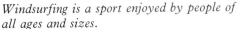

Windsurfing is a sport enjoyed by people of all ages and sizes.

Figure 6 (left): *eleven-year-old Cheri Swatek*

Figure 7 (right:) *Paul Pinkney of New Jersey, aged sixty-six*

hour on average. That includes the fuel to get where you sail from and the depreciation of the wetsuit and board. If like many people you go out twice a week, and maybe a few times in the winter too, the cost can be less than half that. This is an inexpensive sport.

Downhill snow skiing, by comparison, is thirty times more expensive; and water skiing, with boat depreciation and petrol taken into account, is about the same.

This book will give you some information about getting started in the sport, but it is intended to be useful far beyond that. Beginners always ask; how long before I become really good? The answer is: very soon. It usually takes only about thirty hours to have most of the techniques under control. Then you must find something else in the sport at which to be a beginner again, to give yourself a new challenge. There is far more to the sport of windsurfing than just riding a sailboard. You can always try racing, tricks and games, and there is also the continual challenge of trying new locations to sail, each with its own unique conditions and scenery. In the sport of windsurfing there are lots of things to do. You can remain a novice at one aspect or another for years. This book is intended to be a guide to as many facets of this sport as possible, a guide to adventures which are new, exciting and unusual, and which you are sure to find enjoyable.

Chapter Two
Theory of Sailing and Windsurfing

There are many people around – most of whom sail other types of craft – who are certain that windsurfing must be a kind of acrobatic trick that in some way violates basic principles of sailing, if not physics. This chapter aims to enlighten these people and anyone else who is curious about the theoretical mechanics of windsurfing.

Of course, if physics theory is of no interest to you, you do not need to take these next few pages too seriously; you can make your sailboard go just as fast without reading them.

To produce power for propulsion, a sailing-boat or windsurfing sail creates a very special sort of interruption in the flow of the wind. The nature of this interruption and its effects can be most easily illustrated by using the example of another sort of aerofoil – an aeroplane wing – that operates in much the same way as a sail.

As the wind flows over the curved surface which is the top of an aeroplane wing, it has a slightly longer path to travel than the wind which flows underneath along the wing's flat underside. The air that goes over the top of the wing must travel slightly faster than the air which goes underneath, since it must cover a greater distance in the same length of time; for after passage around the wing the air must re-occupy its original space, in order not to leave a vacuum where the wing used to be.

The faster-moving air over the top of the wing gets stretched out over the longer path it must travel. This lowers its pressure, because pressure is proportional to the amount of air in a given location.

Since the air pressure on top of the wing is now less than the air pressure underneath, the wing will try to move upward, pressed by a force proportional to the difference in air pressure between the top and bottom. When the force is great enough, the wing lifts and the aeroplane flies.

A sailing-boat or windsurfing sail is similar to a wing except that: (1) it is vertical rather than horizontal; (2) there is no bottom surface; and (3) the sail does not have a rigid shape. Because of the lack of rigid shape, a sail must be held at a greater angle to the wind in order that wind pressure can inflate the sail into a wing-like shape. The pressure differential produced is similar to that created by an aeroplane wing and has the same effect, tending to draw the sail, and the connected boat or board towards the low-pressure area. This low-pressure area is indicated by the shaded area on the downwind side of the sail in Figure 9.

The pull that a sail creates cannot usually be directed precisely forwards along the sail as one would like, but is pointed somewhat off to the side. This being the case, the boat or board will be drawn sideways if nothing is done about it. To prevent this sideways motion, a plank of wood or plastic called a 'centreboard' or 'daggerboard' is inserted through the hull of the windsurfing board (or boat) in such a way that the plank projects down into the water underneath (see Figure 14, page 22). This board will do little to prevent forward movement, because the board is thin as you look at it front on, but it will

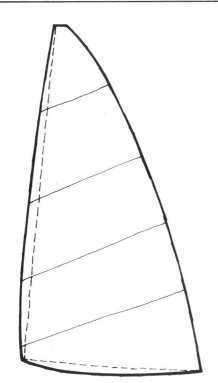 

Figure 8: *Windsurfing sails. There is more cloth area in a sail than would lie flat in a triangle of height and width formed by the mast and booms. The panels of a sail are not straight pieces of* *cloth, but are cut with carefully determined convex edges to produce an airfoil contour when they are sewn together*

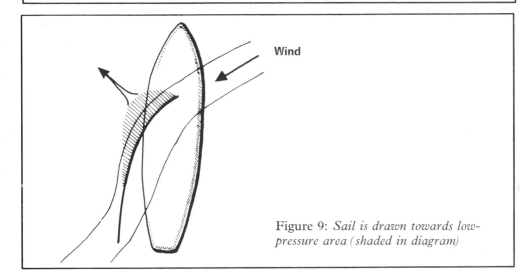

Wind

Figure 9: *Sail is drawn towards low-pressure area (shaded in diagram)*

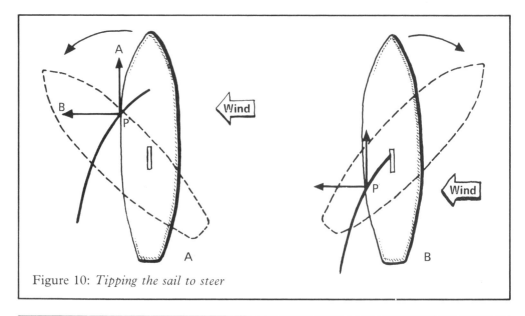

Figure 10: *Tipping the sail to steer*

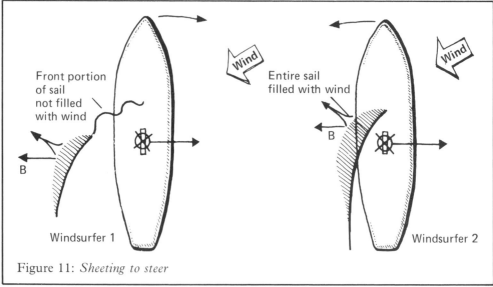

Figure 11: *Sheeting to steer*

greatly reduce sideways movement, since it has a large side area.

If the craft were a sailing boat, there would be one more part: a rudder, with which to deflect water underneath to make the hull turn. However, a sail-powered craft can be steered without a rudder – if the mast is free to tip, as it is on a windsurfing board.

If the sail is raked (tipped) towards the front, the side thrust will tend to turn the board around the daggerboard, pushing the nose downwind and making the board try to align with the wind (see Figure 10(A)).

If the sail is tipped towards the back, the side thrust will turn the board around the daggerboard, pushing the tail further downwind while the nose swings further upwind (see Figure 10(B)).

Simply stated: tipping the sail forwards makes the board turn downwind; tipping the sail back makes it turn upwind.

In Figure 10, the force arrows are shown coming out of the sail at a point P, which is called the 'centre of pressure' of the sail. This point is the imaginary place where one can conceive that all the forces on the sail, from front to back, and top to bottom, act. In reality, this point is not at a constant location, but varies depending on sail trim and wind speed.

In Figure 11 the sail on Windsurfer 1 is rather loosely sheeted – so loosely sheeted that the sail is not filled with wind at the front and is said to be 'luffing'. Windsurfer 2 has its sail tightly sheeted. As can be seen, Windsurfer 1 will have its centre of pressure quite far back (in this case it is behind the daggerboard). This will tend to make the board steer towards the wind just as if its sail were tipped towards the back. Windsurfer 2 will tend to turn in the other direction because the centre of pressure of its sail is forward of the daggerboard.

To sum up:

– To turn a windsurfing board downwind, tip its sail forwards and sheet the sail in.
– To turn a windsurfing board upwind, tip its sail back and sheet the sail out.

There is another way that the sail's pull acts on the windsurfing board. Besides acting on the craft to move it horizontally, the pull also acts in the vertical plane in which you stand.

If there were no wind, you could stand on a board as in Figure 12(A) – sail tipped a bit to one side, body leaning slightly to the other side, and everything in balance.

In a light breeze, you could stand as shown in Figure 12(B), with the sail upright and your body leaning back over the water. In this case, you will feel a pull on your arms proportional to your weight and the angle at which you lean back. For example, if you weigh 75 kilograms (165 pounds) and are leaning back at a 20° angle from the vertical, you will feel a pull of about 19 kilograms (42 pounds), approximately one quarter of your weight. You can experiment with these forces by standing in a doorway with a

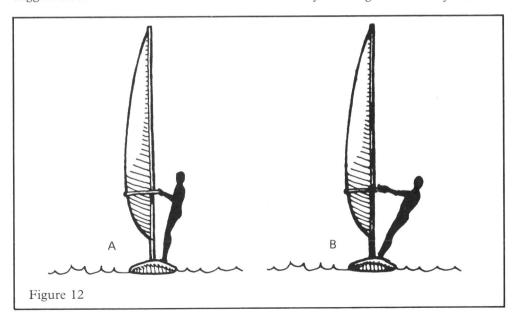

Figure 12

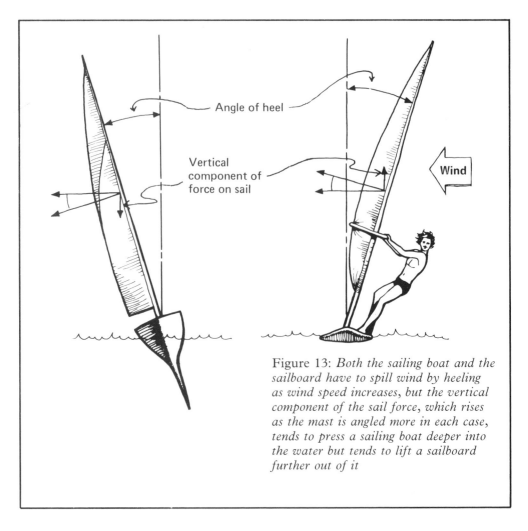

Angle of heel

Vertical component of force on sail

Wind

Figure 13: *Both the sailing boat and the sailboard have to spill wind by heeling as wind speed increases, but the vertical component of the sail force, which rises as the mast is angled more in each case, tends to press a sailing boat deeper into the water but tends to lift a sailboard further out of it*

broomstick across it and leaning back with outstretched arms while holding the broomstick. With your feet directly under the broomstick, you will be leaning at about a 20° angle, which is approximately the angle that you would adopt on a windsurfing board when sailing in a force 3 wind. (See Appendix 4 for a more detailed discussion of these forces.)

If the wind exceeded force 3, you would want to lean your weight even more towards the wind to counterbalance the force on the sail. You can't make your arms any longer, so what you do instead

is allow the sail to 'lean on the wind'. Since your feet are supported by the board, as long as you keep your arms roughly at right angles to your body, the maximum pull you can feel on them will be somewhat more than one half of your body weight.

As the sail is brought over more towards the wind, less and less wind is caught by it. This makes the board ride a bit higher out of the water. In the extreme case where the sailor's back would be completely down on the water (as in a head dip, described in Chapter 8), almost one half of their weight would be borne by the wind. Because some weight is removed from the board, the board rides higher and makes contact with less water, reducing friction between board and water. In terms of speed this will usually more than make up for the loss of wind in the sail due to the sail being lower and having less projected area.

Contrast this situation with the way a sailing boat, with its rigidly connected mast, behaves. As the wind increases, the sailor must lean out further and further to try to sail the boat 'flat'. If the wind is strong enough to start heeling the boat despite the sailor's weight being out over the side, the wind will now be driving the boat somewhat down into the water, tending to slow it down because of water resistance as well as loss of projected sail area (see Figure 13).

These differences between windsurfing boards and sailing boats are not significant in light winds. Most sailing boats have larger daggerboards than windsurfing boards and also have more adjustments available on their sails. In light wind (less than force 4), a sailing boat with a sail of similar size to that of a windsurfing board is equal or superior to a windsurfing board in a race. In a greater wind, however, as the sailing boat heels and the windsurfing board 'leans on the wind', the board comes into its own. So, in winds of force 4 or greater, over a short course (where the physical endurance of the sailor is not a major factor), a windsurfing board cannot usually be beaten on any point of sail by any boat that does not have at least twice the board's sail area.

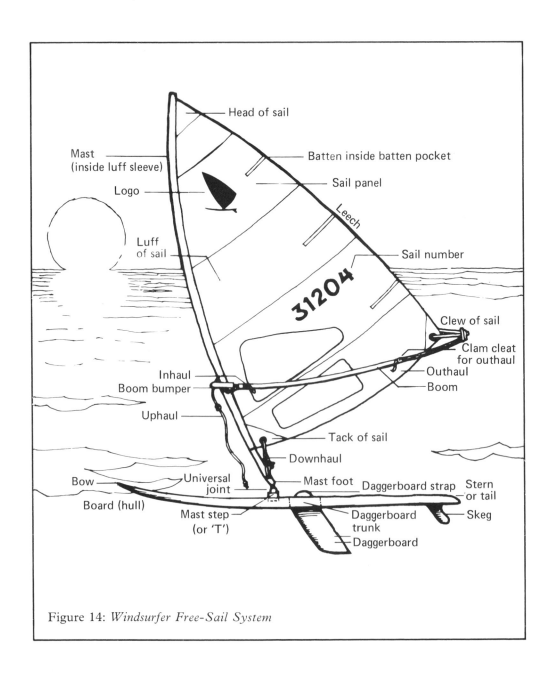

Figure 14: *Windsurfer Free-Sail System*

Chapter Three
Rigging

The standard sailboard free-sail system is a simple device which has only three principal components: the board, the daggerboard and the sail assembly. Figure 14 shows the names of the parts of the craft. The reader is advised to study this diagram to become familiar with the terms before beginning assembly.

Assuming that you begin with a new and completely unassembled sailboard, put your craft together by following the procedure described below.

Sail assembly (the rig)

1 Unassembled, the mast consists of three separate pieces: a mast tip, the mast itself, and a mast base with universal joint assembly attached. As a first step, insert the small wooden or plastic mast tip into the small end of the mast and tape it in place, sealing the joint between the mast tip and the mast with the tape to prevent any water from entering.

2 Slip the sail's luff sleeve (the tube of cloth at the front of the sail) over the mast.

3 Insert the mast base into the bottom of the mast and tie the downhaul line directly from the eyestrap on the base to the tack of the sail. Do not tape the mast foot to the mast.

4 Place the booms around the mast as shown in Figure 17. It is conventional to place the inhaul cleat on the starboard (right) side. Note that the uphaul emerges from the booms from below. Tie one end of the inhaul line

to the D ring with a bowline knot. Now start on the side of the mast nearest the inhaul cleat and run the inhaul line three times around the mast. (Do not go over the tape at the front of the luff sleeve.) Then run the line back through the D ring and into the cleat.

5 With one hand, twist the mast back and forth while pulling on the inhaul between the cleat and the mast with the other hand. This will bring the mast in snugly to the front of the booms. Tighten the line by taking out all of the slack at the cleat.

6 If the booms are on correctly, the uphaul will emerge from the bottom. The uphaul must not come over the rubber boom bumper. If the uphaul is left in this position it will pull off the boom bumper when force is applied to the uphaul while lifting the mast.

7 Blow any sand or dirt out of the outhaul cleat before attaching the outhaul.

8 The outhaul line goes from the boom ends through the clew grommet on the sail, then back around the boom ends again and into the outhaul cleat. To tighten the outhaul, pull back on the clew while pushing forward on the outhaul (see Figure 18).

9 Press the outhaul line into the cleat while applying tension on the line to sink it down into the teeth of the cleat. If the line slips while you are applying tension, there may be dirt in the cleat or the cleat may be worn and need replacement.

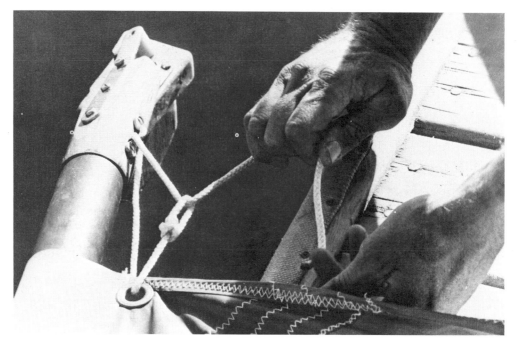

Figure 15 (above): *Tying the downhaul, first step*

Figure 16 (below): *Tying the downhaul, second step. This method of tying the downhaul permits you to tighten it more easily when you are out on the water*

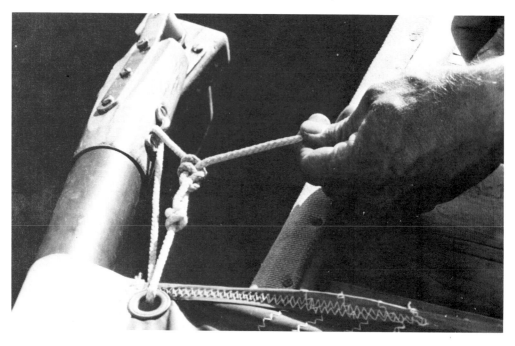

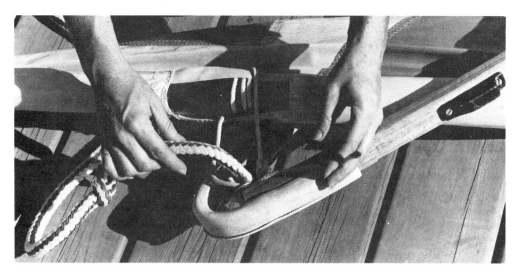

Figure 17 (above): *Wrapping the inhaul onto the mast*

Figure 18 (below): *In order to tighten the outhaul, pull on the clew of the sail with one hand while pushing the outhaul away from you*

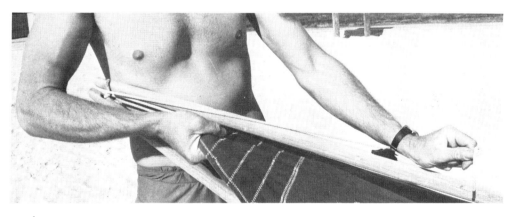

Sail adjustment

For winds up to force 4, first tighten the downhaul just enough to remove any small horizontal wrinkles in the sail panels near the luff sleeve. Next, re-tighten the outhaul so that the clew to boom-end distance is approximately one handspan (the distance from thumb-tip to the tip of little finger when the hand is splayed out). Notice that this means that a smaller person will tighten the outhaul more than a bigger person because a small person's hand will tend to be smaller. Tightening the outhaul generally reduces the sail's power, so this rule gives roughly appropriate amounts of sail power to individuals of different sizes.

For winds exceeding force 4, tighten the outhaul more, roughly halving the clew to boom-end distance at each increase of one Beaufort number (force 5, force 6, etc.). Tightening the outhaul will flatten the sail and reduce its power, thus assisting you in handling higher wind speeds. Strong wind will also tend to

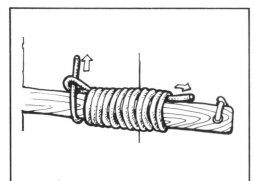

Figure 19: *One way to keep a length of spare line aboard your craft for use in emergencies is to wrap it on the boom as shown*

push the curvature of the sail towards the leech of the sail, which will hinder the sail's ability to go upwind. This can be partly countered by tightening the downhaul somewhat as higher wind speeds are encountered.

Mast-step adjustment

The mast step (T) should fit tightly. Generally speaking, the minimum tightness is that which will barely permit you to lift the entire board by pulling up on the mast. An expert sailor who is sailing in large waves may want the step to fit even tighter. The best way to increase the tightness of the mast-step fit is to spread hot-melt glue (see Chapter 9) on the side of the mast T. A wrap or two of tape will also work, but the tape will require occasional replacement.

If you have trouble removing a mast step from the step well at the end of a sailing session, a screwdriver can be used as a wedge to force the cheek of the T away from the hull. Try to rock the T forwards and backwards, as this motion will tend to loosen it most quickly. It is risky to use the daggerboard as a wedge for the purpose of removing a T, as the daggerboard can be scarred or broken.

Daggerboard fit

The daggerboard should fit tightly enough in its well to stay down when sailing the board *stern first* through the water. You should be able to pull the daggerboard out easily by lifting the daggerboard strap with one hand. On the older daggerboards with rubber stops, cut small amounts from the ends of the rubber stops so that they provide less resistance if the fit is too tight. If any rubber stop is loose in its hole, drive a small finishing nail diagonally through it to hold it in place. On the newer daggerboards equipped with vertical plastic shims, hot-melt glue can be injected under a shim to raise it, or a shim can be popped out and padded with a bit of duct tape to make it a bit higher.

Skeg fit

If a new skeg does not seat easily into the skeg box, file the sides of the skeg's mounting base to reduce its width or length to match the skeg box.

Caution: Whenever you leave your board on a beach where there are children, *always turn it upside down!* Children will *invariably* jump on top of a right-side-up board and play at being 'surfers'. This can break the skeg box.

Chapter Four
Self-Taught Windsurfing

Windsurfing is easy to learn if you get instruction – you can master the basics of the sport in about six hours by attending a windsurfing school. On the other hand, windsurfing can be moderately difficult to learn without instruction. The message is, therefore: if you have access to a school and want to save time, attend the school.

This chapter is intended to help those who have no nearby school, or who own a windsurfing sailboard and have some spare time in which they want to try to teach themselves. Be careful, be patient and *persevere*. With the aid of this chapter, you should be able to teach yourself most of the basics in about three days of one- or two-hour sessions.

Before you begin

When you attempt to learn to windsurf on your own, rapid success will hinge on your being able to set up the best possible situation before going out onto the water. Your objective is to eliminate as many potential difficulties as possible, to enable you to focus undivided attention on simply sailing the craft. This undivided attention is crucial because the first few hours on a sailboard are usually very difficult for an uninstructed beginner. This is not because of a lack of physical ability – any healthy person who weighs more than 30 kilograms (65 pounds) is strong enough to windsurf – but because of the mental adaptation that is required. At first there are many unfamiliar events occurring simultaneously, and your ability to perceive them and respond to them is impaired because your senses are saturated.

When you operate a standard wind-surfing sailboard, you must deal with four basic problems: (1) controlling the force that the wind creates in the sail and learning the art of balancing your weight against that force; (2) steering; (3) controlling the board's roll; and (4) finding the proper courses to sail to avoid obstacles and get where you want to go. As a beginner, your goal is to become so familiar with the first three points that handling them becomes instinctive. Until that happens, you must think about them constantly. In addition, you, like all others who operate sailing craft, must concentrate on point 4.

Not everyone will have trouble with all four points just mentioned. It is useful to have prior knowledge of your assets – to know how your own physique and experience will help you survive your first 'trial by water' on the sailboard. Strong people will find, for example, that they will be able to 'muscle out' of errors, retaining control of the sail's force more easily than a weak or small person can. A small person, on the other hand, won't upset the board so easily when a mistake is made, because in their case stepping off centre doesn't have the same tipping effect as it does with a bigger person. In other words, roll control is easier for small people and harder for big people. Incidentally, people who already know how to surf on waves do not appear to possess any special advantage in initially coping with board roll.

The way a free-sail system is steered is unique, but the principle of mast-rake steering (steering by tipping the mast forward and aft) will be understood by people with prior experience in small high-performance sailing dinghies that have adjustable backstays. The windsurfing simulator used by the windsurfing schools is particularly useful for teaching steering. The simulators also are used to teach sail-force control and the footwork that aids roll control. If you would like to understand the concepts that underlie mast-rake steering, spend some extra time studying Chapter 2.

All successful sailors, no matter what type of craft they are sailing, must understand how to find the proper courses to carry themselves past obstacles and to the places where they wish to go. I call this 'the geometry of sailing'. If you are already a sailor, knowledge of this is already yours. If you are not a sailor, this is one more subject which must be studied and mastered.

Choosing a site

As mentioned earlier, the key to teaching yourself windsurfing is to avoid mental overload by choosing a site which minimizes the problems with which you

Figure 20: *A good beginner's lake in perfect beginner's conditions. The size is limited and it has a dock in deep water on the upwind side*

must deal. You must be able to get back to where you started from: this is the easiest problem to eliminate. Simply pick a very small lake or pond for your first trials so that you can't get very far away from where you began! A pond 100 metres in diameter is large enough, and anything bigger than 200 metres in diameter is too large (see Figure 20).

I experienced two days of frustration and discomfort before I hit on the scheme outlined above. After one trial on a large sea bay and another on a large lake, I finally taught myself on a duck pond about 1 metre deep and about 100 metres across. I have never sailed on anything quite so small since then, but at first that pond was just right for me.

To assist their students in controlling roll, the windsurfing schools use stretches of waveless water and sometimes extra-large daggerboards, which provide high roll resistance. If your beginning site is as small as I recommend and has sloping rather than steep banks, it will tend to remain free of waves. If you cannot find a small pond to use as a self-training site, I recommend that you tether your sailboard. To do this, tie a light line about 30 metres long to the underwater part of the daggerboard of your craft and to the end of a dock on a windward shore. Now, whenever you reach the end

of the line while drifting downwind, you can haul yourself very efficiently back up to the point from which you started.

Watching the wind

On your first day *do not go out* if the wind is greater than force 2 and you have a standard 5.2 square metre (56 square foot) sail; or force 3 if you have a 3.99 square metre (43 square foot) high-wind sail. This will eliminate the problem of having more power in the sail than you can handle. A lighter wind will keep the pull of the sail weak and allow you to make large errors in sail handling without being pulled right off the board. Light wind will also help guarantee that the waves remain small. Force 2 wind is only strong enough to ripple the surface of the water. Again, with a full sail *do not even try* if the wind exceeds force 2. Wait until the next day, or even the next week!

Since they must be able to conduct classes no matter what the weather conditions, windsurfing schools have special small sails for their students to use in winds greater than force 2. These sails keep the students from being overpowered when they mishandle the sail in such winds. Also, students are not permitted to 'graduate' from the simulator and take their first lesson on the water until they show some sail-handling skill. The small sails are described in Chapter 12. They can be purchased from your local dealer.

Getting yourself ready

After having decided on the proper site for your first practice session, your next step is to prepare yourself in whatever ways you can. A wetsuit (see Chapter 10) is advisable not only for reasons of comfort but also to prevent the possibility of hypothermia, often referred to as 'exposure'. This is the condition of excessive heat loss from the body's inner core which results in reduced mobility

and energy output. Hypothermia is not to be taken lightly. In extreme forms it can be fatal.

Also, wear shoes! The rough traction-surface cast into the top of the sailboard's hull makes it possible to sail barefoot, but it is not wise to do so at first. There are several ways in which you can incur minor foot injuries in the first few hours on a sailboard. Wearing a pair of shoes and socks can prevent all such injuries. Specifically, you are guarding against small cuts on the feet and ankles from accidental brushes against the universal joint, and you are also guarding against cuts produced by sharp objects or rocks that you may encounter when you jump off your board. The kind of shoe is important. The best types of shoes for windsurfing are described with other suitable clothing in Chapter 10.

Be sure to check the local regulations – you may need to wear a life jacket. Of course, if you can't swim, you shouldn't be trying to learn to windsurf in the first place. But, if you are just a bit uncertain in the water, I recommend that you wear a life jacket.

You will have to be able to determine the wind direction and make a fairly accurate estimate of the wind speed before making your first foray onto the pond. If the wind is less than force 1, the water's surface may be glassy and only the lightest flags will flutter. This will be fine for your first attempt but, when the wind is this light, you may have to resort to the common sailor's trick of lighting a cigarette – even if you don't smoke – and standing it up on the bank so the smoke will reveal the wind direction. Winds exceeding force 1 will form small ripples on the water, making the wind direction obvious. Do not attempt to sail on your first day (unless you have a small sail) if the ripples are any larger than the ones you can see in Figures 38 to 41 (pages 37 and 38), which indicate a wind speed of about force 2.

Water safety

One of the most important considerations when learning to sail a sailboard is personal safety. I myself have run a windsurfing school for a number of years and have now taught many hundreds of people without any important injury having occurred in any of my classes.

Dangers do exist in this sport, however. Guard against falls in water less than half a metre deep. It is falls of this type that make windsurfing in breaking surf dangerous. It is also hazardous for a beginner to sail too close to shore in a shallow pond. Guard against falls onto other objects, such as docks, buoys or other sailboards. Set yourself a rule in the first six hours of practice: do not attempt to sail away from a dock or buoy; just paddle away. When you are well clear of an obstacle, you can again try to sail. As a beginner, do not sail in a place where there are currents. Do not sail in an offshore wind on any body of water bigger than 8 kilometres (5 miles) in diameter.

Whatever happens, stay with your board. You will always be able to go faster and farther paddling your board than you can by swimming. If you become too tired to paddle, you can lie on the board and wait for help. The board, being white, will be more visible than you would be while swimming. If your sail should become disconnected from the board in a fall, do not swim to the sail; swim to the board. Except in breaking surf, a free-floating, unmanned and unsteered sailboard cannot go as fast as a swimmer, so you should be able to catch your board within 6 metres (20 feet).

Do not abandon your sail rig unless a dire emergency arises which requires that you paddle your board very fast for a long distance. When the sail is attached to your board, it will act as a very effective sea-anchor, slowing your rate of downwind drift. If you wish to make the sail an even more efficient sea-anchor, rest your legs on the mast to submerge the sail as far as possible.

Practise paddling both with the sail rigged and with it unrigged and rolled up. As illustrated in Figures 21 and 22, the windsurfing board can be paddled with the sail still rigged and attached to the board. Sit facing backwards, holding the sail in place with one hand while paddling with the other. Both booms and the top of the mast must be out of the water. This technique will not work in waves higher than about 4 centimetres. In bigger waves, the rig should be disconnected from the board and the sail carefully rolled (see Figure 23). Take your time and do a careful job of rolling the sail, tying it up with the uphaul and outhaul. Place the sail on top of the board, carefully centred; lie on it facing forward and paddle. Practise this in waveless water. It is harder to do than it appears. If you sail often in a place where the wind dies suddenly, it is a good idea to take some small, strong cords along, wrapped on the booms, to help tie up the rig and to strap it down to the board while paddling.

Getting started

Let's assume that you have selected a suitable pond for your first attempt at windsurfing. Now it is time to find a good spot on the pond from which to start. The best place is a dock on the upwind side – the upwind side being the one from which the wind will blow you out to the middle of the pond.

Wind direction

To find the upwind side, you will have to answer the question that one must always ask while sailing: where is the wind coming from? You can look at a flag, at plants bending in the breeze, or at smoke rising and being blown away. You can even judge wind direction a little by feeling the wind blow against your skin.

Figure 21 (top): *When paddling a short distance, drop the sail on the back of the board*

Figure 22 (middle): *The booms should rest on the board and the mast tip and boom ends should be out of the water. Paddle facing backwards, holding the sail with one hand*

Figure 23 (bottom): *When paddling a long distance or in small waves, roll the sail and lay it along the top of the board. Remove the daggerboard for better steering and place it under the sail*

A particularly accurate method of determining wind direction – one that is available to a sailboarder in all but the lightest winds – is to hold the mast upright with the uphaul and observe which way the wind blows the sail. The far edge of the sail will point straight downwind if the mast is held perfectly vertical.

Courses relative to the wind

A sailing boat or sailboard can be sailed in certain directions through the wind but not in all directions. You can sail *with* the wind – i.e., downwind; this is called 'running'. You can sail *across* the wind, at right angles to it, in either direction; this is called 'reaching'. You can even point the nose of your craft somewhat upwind, about 45°; this is called 'beating'. But you cannot point it upwind any higher. If you try to do this, the boat or sailboard will stop, the sail

will begin to fill on the wrong side, and you will start going sideways or even backwards. This is called a stall. It occurs on a sailboard whenever you try to point the nose into the never-never land that lies between 45° of either side of straight upwind.

What if you want to sail to a place that is upwind from where you are? In this case, try to go as much upwind as you can without stopping or slowing down to a stall. When you encounter an obstacle, change direction to go as much upwind as you can while standing on the other side of the sail. Keep doing this until you reach your goal.

First time out

When you have rigged your sail, you are ready to go. Toss the sail out as far as you can. Launch your board off the dock or wade out with it into deep water. Insert the daggerboard with

Figure 24 (top): *Rig the sail as described in Chapter 3*

Figure 25 (middle): *Carry the sail with the mast towards the wind, the boom resting on your shoulder*

Figure 26 (bottom): *Keeping the mast towards the wind, pitch the sail like a javelin*

Figure 27 (top left): *Throw the sail horizontally*, not *upwards*

Figure 28 (top right): *Carry the board to the water, standing on the top side with one hand on the step well, the other in the daggerboard slot*

Figure 29 (middle): *Insert the daggerboard into its well with the point towards the back of the hull*

Figure 30 (bottom right): *Paddle out to the sail, kneeling, face forward*

Figure 31 (bottom left): *Pick up the mast step from the water and press it into place with the heels of both hands. If it is very tight, you can step on it once you have stood up, to drive it in the entire way. Then take hold of the uphaul*

33

Figure 32 (above): *When you first stand up, place your front foot just ahead of the mast step, your rear foot on the centre of the daggerboard; be sure your arches are on the board's centreline*

Figure 33 (below): *As the board swings round to leave the sail on the downwind side, go slowly up the uphaul, hand over hand*

the point of the daggerboard towards the tail of the hull, and climb aboard. Paddle out to the sail; then pick up the mast step and plug it into the board (see Figures 24 to 31).

Take hold of the uphaul, swing the mast round so it is at right angles to the board and, keeping your weight on the board's centreline, get to your feet. Place one foot just in front of the mast, the other across the daggerboard. Your feet should point straight across the board with the centreline of the board right under your arches (see Figure 32). Pull and lean against the uphaul a little to steady yourself. Begin to experiment with the roll of the board and the swing of the mast by pulling the sail one way and the other with the uphaul, leaving the sail down in the water the entire time.

It is very likely that the wind will be blowing towards you from the side the sail is on (sailboards tend to drift into this position when their sails are lowered). When you are sailing, your back will always be towards the wind, and thus you will have to get the sail round to the downwind side of your board.

There are two ways of getting your sail to the other (downwind) side. One is slow but sure, the other quick and (at first) uncertain! The first method involves lifting the sail slightly (so the top of the mast is about 1 metre above the surface of the water), while keeping the mast at a perfect right angle to the board. Then wait for the wind to catch the sail and slowly turn the sail, the board and yourself right round. The sail will eventually become the most downwind part of the sailboard (see Figure 33). The second method is quicker, but you are likely to tip over when you first try it. In this method (Figure 34), pull the mast towards the board using the uphaul. Then, using the

Figure 34 (above): *A faster way of getting the sail to the downwind side is to pull it across the board mast first, using the uphaul*

Figure 35 (right): *Keep stepping your feet around as the sail comes across the board*

Figure 36: *Finish with the mast at right angles to the board*

uphaul, drag the mast over the board, not lifting the sail. Keep facing the sail and keep moving your feet to stay out of the way of the mast as it comes across the board. Step carefully so you don't tip the board.

When the mast is on the downwind side, pick up the sail very slowly, using the uphaul. Keep the mast at *a perfect right angle* to the side of the board. Reach across to the back boom (the boom closest to the tail of the board) with your front hand (the hand closest to the front of the board) (see Figure 37). Grasp the boom about 15 centimetres away from the mast with either an underhand or an overhand grip. (Small people are usually more comfortable with an underhand front-hand grip; taller people usually prefer an overhand grip.)

Now draw the mast across the centreline of the board toward the upwind side, keeping the bottom edge of the sail at *a perfect right angle* to the edge of the board. Reach out with the hand that is nearest the back of the board and grab the boom about a shoulder's width distance down the boom from your front

hand (see Figure 38). Gently push the mast forwards about 30 centimetres towards the point of the board's nose, and follow that movement with a gentle pull in towards yourself with your back hand. Pull your back hand in about 30 centimetres (1 foot) (see Figure 39).

The board should start moving forward in a straight line. If it starts to turn downwind, tip the mast back a bit towards your face. If the board starts to turn upwind, pull your back hand in a few centimetres towards the centre and tip the mast a similar distance towards the nose of the board. Keep the mast over the centreline; do not allow it to lean downwind. A helpful practice at first is always to keep your front arm bent while sailing in a straight line. Keep watching your front arm and re-bend it every time you relax and let it straighten (see Figure 40).

Controlling the sail's force

If a gust hits you and you feel yourself being pulled towards the sail, push out, away from the side of the board, with your back hand, keeping your front arm bent! If the gust pulls very hard, let go with your back hand. You will be strongly tempted at first to let go with

Figure 37: *Reach across to the rear boom with the hand that is nearest the front of the board. Then draw the mast across the centreline with the front hand, keeping the bottom edge of the sail at a* perfect right angle *to the board*

Figure 38: *The rear hand is placed on the boom a shoulder's width from the front hand. Rather than bend (as in the photo), draw the mast further to windward before grasping with the rear hand.*

Figure 40: *Once you are on a straight course, concentrate on keeping your mast on the centreline or to windward. At first, think of always keeping your front arm bent. Lean back against the pull of the sail and push the board ahead with a straight front leg*

Figure 39: *To start, tip the sail towards the nose of the board as you pull in with your back hand. Slightly flexed knees will give a beginner more stability*

your front hand. *Don't!* At least, never let go with your front hand unless you let go with your back hand at the same instant. If you feel yourself falling away from the sail, pull in *fast* with your back hand.

When recovering from one of your inevitable first falls, always rearrange the bottom edge of the sail at right angles to the board before trying to start sailing again. Don't rush. Take your time and think. As things begin to make sense, they will start to become automatic.

Steering

Try some gentle S turns. Tip your mast and sail towards the nose of the board and pull in towards yourself a bit with your back hand. You will turn downwind. To turn upwind, tip the mast back a bit, keeping your front arm bent and straightening your back arm. Think of the sail as a scoop. When you tip the scoop forward and catch the wind going across your board at right angles to your course, the wind will pull the nose of the board downwind. When you put your scoop towards the back, the tail of the board will be pulled downwind. With your back hand, angle the scoop so that it encounters the wind as effectively as possible.

Turning round

At some time you will have to make a turn. Do it at least 30 metres from the nearest obstacle. For starters, try coming about and gybing by using just the uphaul. These operations, known as making a 'rope tack' and making a 'rope gybe', are both very easy.

To make a 'rope tack' (an upwind turn),* let go of the boom slowly with your back hand and grab the uphaul with

*The popular term among sailboarders for coming about while using the uphaul is 'rope tack'. In sailing, the term 'tack' can mean a downwind turn but sailboarders usually use the word 'gybe' exclusively for this and use the word 'tack' for upwind turns.

this hand. Now let go of the boom with your front hand. Using the uphaul only, and not touching the booms, tip the sail toward the tail of the board and begin taking small steps around the mast to get to the other side. Constantly face the sail and try to keep your feet close to the mast base. Don't go too far forward or the nose of the board will submerge! Keep the end of the booms just above the water to make the board turn as fast as possible. Don't touch the booms until you have moved completely round to the other side! (see Figure 41). Now, just as

Figure 41: *To make a 'rope tack', let go of the boom with the rear hand first. Then grasp the uphaul with both hands. Tip the sail toward the rear and walk around the* front *of the mast, taking small steps. Do not touch the booms* until the sail is at right angles to the board on the new side

before, arrange the bottom edge of the sail so it is at right angles to the board; reach across with what is now your front hand to what is now your back boom, and with that hand raise the mast across the centreline. Reach out with your back hand and, just as before on the other side, tip the mast toward the nose with your front hand and then pull in a bit with your back hand.

To make a 'rope gybe' (a downwind turn), slowly let go of the boom with your back hand and grab the uphaul with this hand. Then let go with your front hand and start tipping the mast towards the front of the board. When the sail is pointing directly forwards along the board, pivot on the ball of your rear foot until it aligns with the axis of the board, your toes pointing forward. Then bring your front foot back to the rear foot so that both feet are side by side atop the daggerboard, with toes pointing towards the nose of the board. Now, very quickly, step forwards with the foot that is to be your front foot as you continue to swing the sail across the nose of the board. Then position your feet in the usual places, one in front of the mast step, one over the daggerboard. Again, don't touch the booms until the sail is once more at right angles to the board.

Downwind sailing

After some practice on turns and on upwind and crosswind (reaching) courses, you should try going directly downwind (a running course). First try the 'luffing' technique. This is easy. Just hold the uphaul and tip the sail towards the front. The board will drift downwind, pulled by the drag of the wind on the loose sail and your body. Steer by leaning the sail to the right or left of the centreline.

To sail downwind, start to head off downwind by raking the mast forward and pulling in with your back hand. Now swing the mast round over the windward side of the board, but continue to pull in

Figure 42: *Head downwind by tipping the sail forward and pulling in with your back hand, then swing the mast round over the side of the board toward the old windward side. Step back with both feet as you do when gybing*

hard with your back hand. Pivot your rear foot so the toe faces forwards (as you do when gybing). Bring your front foot back alongside your rear foot, standing so that your toes are pointed directly forward. The toes of both feet should be no further forwards than the centre of the daggerboard well. The final position you adopt should see the booms at right angles to the board with the wind at your back (see Figure 42).

If a gust hits you while you are on a downwind course, don't let the sail 'out' (forward) with your back hand (the hand furthest from the mast)! Instead pull *back* with the mast hand. This will have the same effect on the sail as letting out with the back hand, and it will help to keep your body weight aft, which will make it easier for you to stay balanced. If you keep the mast tipped back behind its base, gusts will have less effect on your balance and will tend to keep the board moving faster.

To steer to the left while going downwind, tip the sail to the *right* and

Figure 43a (left): *To turn right, lean the mast left and pull in with the right hand*

Figure 43b (right): *Similarly, to turn left, tip the sail right and pull in with the left hand*

pull the boom toward your face with your *left* hand. To steer toward the right, tip the sail *left* and pull with your *right* hand. Try to keep the sail at a true right angle to the wind at all times (see Figure 43a and b).

When you return to a reaching course from a running course, remember to step up with the foot that is going to become the front foot.

Keeping the nose from diving

When you have gained a bit of confidence, shift your front foot round so that, instead of being in front of the mast, it is positioned beside the mast, with the toe pointed somewhat forwards in the line of travel. Figure 44 on page 42 shows both the beginner foot position and the advanced foot position. Start trying to lean back, away from the pull of the sail. Push the board ahead with your front foot, keeping your front leg straight. Consciously try to lean back over the water – the same way a waterskier leans away from a tow rope.

When you first begin sailing the board, it is important for you to concentrate on keeping your front arm *bent* – because it is easier for a beginner to remember to keep an arm bent than for him to remember to keep the mast near the centreline of the board or, if necessary, windward of the centreline, which is the effect that bending the front arm produces. After about four to six hours on the board, your understanding of how the mast moves and your automatic reactions should be developed well enough to leave your front arm straight most of the time. You will find that leaving the front arm straight considerably relieves the strain on the muscles of this arm.

Shoulder roll

The key point to remember now is: *never let the mast go to leeward* (the downwind side of the board). Whenever it starts to get across to the leeward side of the centreline, push *out* with the back hand and simultaneously pull *down* with the front hand. This motion is called the 'shoulder roll' – it will produce a roll of the front shoulder towards the wind. Pulling the mast lower in this way allows your front leg to get a better driving angle on the board. When you pull in your back hand to stop the shoulder roll, you will feel an instant acceleration.

Now you have the basics of wind-surfing. Practise all of these manoeuvres by going around a triangular course. When you have had approximately twenty hours of practice on your board, it will be time for you to go on to the advanced techniques described in Chapter 6.

Chapter Five
Windsurfing School Techniques

Windsurfing is a sport which is easily taught if the instructor uses a well-considered lesson plan, is attentive to the students, and applies a few tricks of the trade. Attentiveness and patience with students are qualities that an instructor usually has or doesn't have, but the other two factors can be acquired, since well-polished lesson plans and a number of clever tricks have emerged from the several hundred professional schools teaching windsurfing in Europe and North America. In what follows I will describe how I teach classes of three or four students, the typical size of windsurfing classes in the United States.

Incidentally, even if you do not plan to become a professional windsurfing instructor, knowing how the standard classes are conducted may help you to see the task you face as a beginner or help you when you try teaching your friends.

I open my classes with a brief interview in which I ask the students if they have had any experience in downhill skiing, surfing or sailing. The tone in which a student replies is as important as the answer itself. An extremely confident reply, such as 'I am a really good surfer', usually marks a student who will be inattentive. That person may feel he or she already knows it all. The most difficult students are overconfident surfers; the easiest to teach are downhill skiers. A student who has sailed and

skied is usually going to be a quick learner. If someone comes across in an overconfident manner, I arrange it so that that individual is the last one in the class to try each manoeuvre. This enables the overconfident person to see other students having problems, and such observation will cause less embarrassment if that person has problems too.

After the interview, it is wise to give a brief history of windsurfing, followed by a listing of the parts of the craft and the rarer materials of which they are made (polyethylene, epoxy fibreglass, teakwood), which always intrigues students. These topics are included in the lesson plan and covered early in order to head off any ill-timed questions later in the class when I am teaching techniques for actually using the equipment.

I next describe, in the simplest possible terms, how to determine the wind direction – by using the sail, by feel, and by watching the small waves (as discussed in Chapter 4). I follow that with a quick talk on upwind sailing, stressing how a student should steer the sailboard so that the small waves come at the board at a 45° angle.

I always use a simulator when giving windsurfing instruction. In fact, I would not teach without this apparatus. A student who is first instructed on a simulator already knows how to steer a sailboard when first trying to sail on the water. A student who does *not* learn on a simulator usually becomes confused when first out on the water, and quite often will tire from constant falling before

Figure 44: *When the student first goes onto the water, the teacher should sail near by, downwind, describing each manoeuvre*

finally discovering the trick of tipping the sail correctly to steer.

The windsurfing simulator is designed to simulate some of the motions of a sailboard. When using a simulator, first demonstrate each manoeuvre by performing it yourself. Then get each student to try the manoeuvre, get another person to try and come back to the first student later. If you proceed from manoeuvre to manoeuvre and student to student quickly, no one will become bored.

If an instructor keeps touching a student or the student's sail rig rather than trying to talk the student into placing the sail in the right positions, the student will not feel the sensations that are associated with the different sail positions and will not learn the correct positions as quickly. Touching the student or the sail rig while a student is on the simulator is, therefore, to be avoided.

If the wind is gusty, however, you *should* hold onto the uphaul about 25 centimetres (10 inches) below the booms. This will protect the student from a fall onto the ground if a gust hits and the student doesn't open his or her back hand. If you stand just to windward when the student is on the simulator, you will be able to use your knee to prevent the board from turning abruptly upwind if the student doesn't sheet in properly. Failure to sheet in correctly is a very common problem with beginners.

After teaching all the students how to sail on the same tack on the simulator, teach them the foot manoeuvres used in rope gybing. First, get all the students to walk through these foot manoeuvres in unison on the ground, then ask each one to try it individually on the simulator. After each student has gybed and switched the sail to the other side of the board, teach that student how to sail on that tack using the same techniques used on the previous tack.

Each student finishes on the simulator

by coming about once or twice by using the uphaul only. Make sure that the students understand the difference between coming about and gybing. Coming about is used for going upwind, while gybing is used for going downwind. This seems to be a point of considerable confusion to beginners.

As each student goes out on the water, it is necessary to watch them carefully for a few minutes and to offer step-by-step guidance. This is because the initial excitement often makes the student suddenly forget all the simulator instruction.

If you are teaching in an area that is unbounded on one side, or if you are teaching more than three students at the same time, tether the windsurfing boards (tie short anchor lines to their daggerboard wells) for the first hour or so of practice, to keep the students in a restricted area. This method is commonly used at schools where the number of lessons is such that it justifies the time and expense of providing permanently placed anchors for the tethers.

The best windsurfing instructors are those who can keep responding to their student's manoeuvres, offering small corrections when they are needed, and heading off difficulties before they become so severe that they lead to a fall. If a student doesn't respond properly to a command, he or she may simply not have understood all the terms used. Therefore, repeat the command using different words. If the student still doesn't respond, repetition or voicing the

Figure 45: *When following a student on the water, the instructor should stay astern and keep out of the student's wind. Note the difference between the instructor's foot position and the student's. The latter is better for a beginner because it helps maintain roll stability. As the student progresses, the more flexible position used here by the instructor should be adopted*

command more forcefully often works.

When you are out on the water with your students, it is important to stay close to them so that they can hear your commands, yet you must stay out of their paths and not interfere with their wind. At first you should stay slightly to windward and astern of a student; then, as the student's skill increases and he or she is not falling so often, move in directly astern. As a last step, to help a student perfect details in his or her technique, pass your student (to leeward), give the command 'copy me', and sail directly ahead of the student.

A very small sail called the 'mini' sail is useful for teaching in high winds (over force 3), especially when used in conjunction with a specially constructed, extra-long daggerboard. The long daggerboard slows the roll rate and allows teaching in the larger waves associated with strong wind. A long daggerboard is also useful when teaching large people to sail, since such people usually have more severe roll-stability problems.

In the second session with your class, you should briefly demonstrate on the simulator how to turn to head directly downwind and how to steer while going downwind. Just before the students go out on the water, they should also be taught the basic right-of-way rules (see Appendix 3).

Once the students are out of the water, they should be encouraged to sail one or two complete circuits around a triangular course set out in the teaching area. At this stage, students who appear truly proficient should be issued with larger sails.

Above all, keep the class lively and fun. Try not to get bogged down in pedantry or technical detail. The best way to teach windsurfing is to get your students to go out and try it – which is what they all want to do anyway.

Chapter Six
Advanced Windsurfing Techniques

I have sailed windsurfing sailboards on canals in Europe, on the Gulf of Mexico, on the Pacific Ocean near Tahiti, and in the English Channel. Sailing windsurfing boards in novel places is a hobby of mine. It is exciting – I like the adventure. But I have found that the experience is enjoyable only when my windsurfing skills are sufficient for me to handle the wind and wave conditions that I encounter.

Wind and waves vary, and in some places both can change very rapidly. The techniques discussed in this chapter are those that you will need to cope with the more challenging conditions away from the smooth waters on the beginner's pond where you first learned to sail your craft. You must master these techniques before you go out in certain areas, or you will not have a good time (at best)—or may need rescue (at worst).

The type of place in which you sail determines the minimum level of skills you must possess. A lake that is 1 or 2 kilometres across can become choppy with waves created by boats and wind, but the waves will rarely exceed a quarter of a metre in height. If you take precautions against exposure, you will be as safe on such a lake as on your beginner's pond, but you will have fun sailing there only if you can handle the wind.

A large bay or harbour may have waves up to one metre in height, and may also have heavy vessel traffic. You must have the skill to handle such waves and avoid the traffic.

The sea and very large bays or lakes have waves up to several metres in height, and swells also, but as far as you are concerned their most important characteristic is that there's only one shoreline – the one from which you started. Sail on such bodies of water only if your skill level is sufficient to handle wind and waves far greater than those in which you start. In other words, you should always have something in reserve. Otherwise, if conditions change, you may have a long paddle back in. Rivers and some bays and estuaries have currents as well as waves and boat traffic. Your skills under these conditions must include some understanding of geometry to enable you to calculate how to get from point A to point B while the current is moving you sideways towards obstacle C.

Higher winds

When you first tackle winds exceeding force 4 (15 knots) you should do so on a small, land-enclosed body of water with unobstructed wind. In other words, on the day you first see the larger tree branches bend and swing, go back to your beginner's pond.

In force 4 wind on a small pond, you will see black ruffled areas appear on the water's surface when the wind gusts. These marks, as well as the tossing of the larger trees, indicate the wind speed.

Start out from a shore which has the wind blowing parallel to it. Make sure that there is a shore downwind projecting out within a couple of kilometres. This 'lee shore' will catch you should problems arise.

Wear a wetsuit, and don't forget to wear boat shoes on this first attempt.

You may have to do some walking! Be sure that your mast step is tight in the board. Wrap some plastic tape around the mast step T to improve the fit, if the T is at all loose.

Getting started in a strong wind is the beginner's biggest problem. When the proper steps are not followed, the sailboard turns on the novice and faces nose up into the wind, stubbornly resisting all the influence of a forward-raked mast. This seems to happen to most people the first time they attempt to get started with a standard sail in winds greater than force 3; I call it the 'force 4 barrier'.

What will get you beyond the barrier is acquiring the trust that the basic starting procedure will work more effectively in this stronger wind *if you change the order of the steps*. So lean to windward, and let yourself start falling back. Fall towards the water *first*. Pull in with your back hand on the way down. If you pull in hard, the wind will buoy you up and away you will go! It is unnatural; you have to *believe* that when you pull in you will stop falling towards the water. A person who has learned to do this has learned the essence of the art of windsurfing. All other techniques are

Figure 46: *Daggerboard sailing at its best*

only refinements of that art.
Points to concentrate on are:

1 Don't hold the boom too close to the mast. The greater the wind speed, the further back from the mast you must put your front hand. First try it with your hand about 25 centimetres back from the mast. Experiment with overhand and underhand grips.

2 Don't let your front foot get too far forward. In fact, in higher winds it is best to keep it alongside the mast step. If your foot goes forwards, you will make a submarine out of your sail-board by forcing the nose underwater.

3 Don't be timid! Start to fall toward the wind, but before falling too far, *yank* towards yourself with your back hand. If there is enough wind, you won't keep falling – you will start going up and forward. In fact, at first, you may occasionally get catapulted right over the nose of your craft. Good! That shows you are pulling in forcefully with the back hand. Don't pull in quite so hard next time, though. Let me emphasize once again: *don't be timid!* In deep water you can't get hurt in the above manoeuvre. If you pull in too hard, you will just go flying through the air to a soft splashdown. When I was going through this phase, I thought those falls were super – much better than those limp crumples onto the board that I'd had as a raw novice. The mark of timidity is a fall to windward; the mark of over-aggressiveness or error in wind-speed calculation is a fall over the bow. Better the latter than the former. When you are going over the nose, you are starting to catch on.

4 Keep your body straight. In other words, don't bend at the waist. Drive the board ahead with a straight front leg. Bend your back leg for comfort and balance.

Now, feel yourself hanging from the sail, which is held in place by the wind. Let yourself drop down until you are parallel to the water, mere centimetres above it. Let your back slap a wave or two, then pull in and fly back up. You've done it! This is the essence of real windsurfing.

Reading the water

Part and parcel of being an 'expert' sailboarder is falling less often than a beginner does. Nothing will prevent falls so effectively as foreknowledge of what the wind is about to do in the exact spot where you are sailing. The method of obtaining such foreknowledge is this: simply look at the water about 5 metres ahead and about 5 metres to windward of your bow – the colour of the water there can tell you much about the wind that is about to hit you. Simply put: if the water in that spot is smoother, brighter and shinier than the water elsewhere, then you are about to encounter a momentary lull – sheet in! If the water is darker, more 'ruffled', then there is a gust coming, so get ready to do a 'shoulder roll'.

Observe other windsurfers who are ahead and to windward of your craft. If someone who you *know* is better than you suddenly falls up there, get ready for some radical wind changes! I've used this technique several times during races to pass folks who are usually my betters.

Fast tacking

In racing, the 'fast tack' is far superior to the beginner's method of coming about (the 'rope tack'). The most important reason for learning the fast tack, however, is to be able to handle waves better.

When executing a rope tack, you momentarily disconnect yourself from the sail power and are left with nothing to lean against. During this time the only stability you have is from your body balance on that unstable board. Even when you are sailing in moderate waves, it can sometimes be difficult to rope tack

Figure 47: *To start a fast tack, tip the sail down to the water at the back and pull in strongly with the back hand*

Figure 48: *Bring both hands together. Step forward with your front foot*

Figure 49: *Pull the bow of the board through the wind by sheeting the sail right against your rear leg*

Figure 50: *Step forward so both toes point aft, and reach for the boom on the other side*

Figure 51: *Halfway through the tack, the toes of both feet are right at the mast step facing directly aft*

without taking a brief swim in the process.

You should not attempt many fast tacks until you have about twenty hours of practice on your board. Fast tacking requires sensitive adjustments in board banking. It takes some time to get the feel of making such adjustments.

When you are ready to try fast tacking, go out on your beginner pond when the wind is moderate, about force 3.

Below – in numbered lists indicating simultaneous actions – are step-by-step instructions for executing a fast tack. As you read these instructions, study the photos carefully (see Figures 47 to 51) to get an impression of the dynamics of this manoeuvre.

Sail and hands	*Feet*
1 Continue to sail in a straight line.	1 Move your front foot across in front of the mast to get the toe positioned just to the leeward side of the centreline.
2 Rake your mast well back – so far back that the end of the boom goes underwater.	2 Lean slightly on your back foot. This raises the bow and makes it come across the wind faster.
3 Pull in hard with your back hand, bringing the bottom edge of the sail right against your leg. The board will cross the eye of the wind. Extend your front arm to lean the mast away and to leeward. (The sail has not crossed the wind yet, and will still be drawing wind from the original side.)	3 Lean your weight forward onto the ball of your forward foot.
4 Slide your back hand up to your front hand.	4 Bring your back foot up, pivoting on the ball of your front foot and plant your feet side by side, toes pointing dead aft. Your toes should be right next to the front of the mast step.
5 Reach across to the boom on the opposite side with the hand that will become your back hand.	5 Put your weight on the ball of the foot that is about to become your front foot.
6 Grip the new side boom with what is now your front hand; then slide your back hand down the boom and pull in with it, raking the mast forward.	6 Pivot on the ball of what is now your front foot, swinging the rear foot down the board to its position just behind the daggerboard well.

The most common error in executing a fast tack is failing to step forward *smartly* in step 4 above. Beginners look just fine up to that point – the sail pulled against the leg, etc. Then they freeze. The next thing that happens is a fall to windward as if the beginner were poleaxed.

You *must*: move your feet after the bow has crossed the wind. Don't take small steps, take large ones. You will rock the boat a lot, but the key to success is to change sides so fast that, even if you are falling, you will have the sail inflated and pulling again on its new side to correct any balance problems.

Sometimes people don't tip the sail back far enough or fast enough, or sheet in quickly enough on the original side, and the board turns so slowly that the rhythm is lost. Rhythm is the key. When young Matt Schweitzer (twice a world champion) fast tacks, his movements are so rhythmic that the entire manoeuvre looks like dancing.

When going from one reach to the other reach, rather than from a beat to a beat, really lean on your back leg. It's incredible how fast you can make the sailboard tack if you do this.

Tip-top sailors often actually jump aft with both feet. This kicks the nose up to a 45° angle and makes the board execute an instant about-turn. A very impressive manoeuvre.

There are several variations on the hand and foot movements of the fast tack. Some people grab the boom on the new side with the hand that will be their new front hand. Others grasp the mast itself or, briefly, the uphaul, with the new front hand to bring the mast back and forward. Try different methods and watch others during races.

Many sailboarders practise a kind of jump around the mast that actually gets both feet in the air momentarily. This tack takes less time to execute than any other tack, which makes it very useful in

big waves. It jostles the board quite a bit as you land, however, which is undesirable when racing in light winds. It's a very good tack for show when, after much practice, you can do it in the twinkling of an eye.

Gybing

There are many ways to gybe a windsurfing board. The method you select is determined by the radius of the turn you are trying to make, the wind speed and the wave conditions.

Rope gybe

The 'rope gybe' described in Chapter 4 can be used to make quite a small radius turn. The key is to let the sail out further with the uphaul, and to lean the sail as far out to windward as possible. After you have come around, a quick yank on the uphaul will bring the booms up to where you can grab them again.

This technique works well in reasonably high wind but isn't effective in light wind. It's unstable in waves. In a race, while rounding a mark in the company of other competitors, you may have to execute this gybe very carefully and conservatively; otherwise you may clobber someone with your wide-flung sail.

Power gybe

Another gybe – one that's particularly effective for close quarters in light winds and flat water – is the 'power gybe', (see Figures 52 to 55). This differs from the rope gybe in that you do not move your feet back. Remain in place while you reach round to the far side of the sail with the front hand and smoothly pull the far boom around the front while keeping the mast nearly vertical (raked back if the wind is fairly strong). The radius of turn can be further decreased by leaning the mast aft after the sail has crossed the board's centreline.

Figure 52: *A power gybe is useful at close quarters in light winds. To start it, reach around the mast to the lee-side boom*

Figure 53: *Pull the board around by drawing in on the lee-side boom*

Figure 54: *Keep your feet well aft as in the other gybes or as when you are sailing downwind*

Figure 55: *Step forward when the gybe is complete*

Figure 56: *A variation on the power gybe is the 'stop turn', which will bring your board to a complete halt and then cause it to gybe in the reverse direction*

Figure 57: *Continue to push on the boom while leaning the mast aft. The board will gybe*

Figure 58: *Another gybe is the 'sailing-boat gybe'. The sail is tipped forward and the booms are passed overhead*

Figure 59: *The gybe is rarely used except in light winds while racing in crowded quarters*

By-the-lee gybe

This is an elegant manoeuvre. You can't possibly make a tight turn by using it, but it is a highly successful gybe for high winds and big waves. Therefore, it is important to master it. This gybe is very simple: just keep pointing the board further and further downwind and finally through to the other tack. Keep the sail on the same side. Move your feet back and then forwards again, just as you do when rope gybing. Eventually, the board will be across the wind and the sail will be backwards or 'by-the-lee'. Flip the sail round when you feel ready, and the manoeuvre is completed. It's that simple. Try not to touch the uphaul. Just like the fast tack, this gybe 'leaves the power on' for the maximum length of time. It is possible to stay on a plane continuously while doing it.

In very high winds

When first you venture out in winds well over force 4, for example in force 6 (25 knots or so), you will encounter some new problems. Sailing upwind is tiresome; before long, your arms almost want to drop off. Off the wind, something really strange starts to happen: the side of the board rises up, and then the board flips over onto its back!

What is going on? First of all, upwind you are encountering 'drag', the evil antagonist of sailing boats, supersonic aeroplanes, rockets re-entering the earth's atmosphere and sailboards. On courses off the wind, we have something peculiar mainly to sailboards: 'daggerboard plane'. Once you have discovered the joy of going downwind, it's easier to accept the difficulty of going upwind – so I'll first describe how to deal with the problem that arises in high-speed, downwind sailing.

The downwind challenge

'Daggerboard plane' is a term used to describe that situation when the daggerboard is starting to act like a planing water ski. You accidentally roll the board a little while it's going very fast, and the next thing you know the daggerboard is trying to plane to the surface. If the daggerboard makes it to the surface, the hull has to be riding on its edge and you'll have a tough time staying aboard.

When the daggerboard is not presenting too great a tendency to plane up, you can handle this problem by attempting to hang on to the precarious balance you do have – keeping one foot on either side of the centreline of the board, and jamming down on an uprising rail (edge of the board) to get the board level again. As speed increases the nose lifts further, leaving more and more of the front of the hull out of the water and intensifying the daggerboard plane, making the nose swing and the board yaw. Finally, when the waterline is nearly back to the daggerboard, the action of the hull becomes too radical to deal with by simple weight adjustment. At this point you must resort to luffing or turning upwind, in order to slow down and regain control lest you fall. In choppy water these problems occur even sooner.

Faced with the problem of daggerboard plane, many recreational windsurfers choose to change to a reduced and aft-raking daggerboard. This moves the centre of lateral resistance back to make it easier to head off (turn downwind), and leaves the daggerboard area insufficient to plane up the hull. Aft-raking daggerboards are not stock equipment on a Windsurfer board and are not legal in racing, so I'll discuss them later, in Chapter 12.

The all-round solution, legal in racing in all classes, and absolutely necessary whenever you want to go downwind on any sailboard in *very* high wind, is to learn to sail with the daggerboard completely out.

1 Wear slit-sole boat shoes. They help you grip the rails.

2 Don't bother to try to sail without a daggerboard unless wind speed is steadily over force 4.

3 Holding the boom only with the front hand (some 30 centimetres behind the mast), position the bottom edge of the sail so that this edge is at right angles to the edge of the hull, or even a bit forward of that position.

4 Crouch, and with your rear hand grab your daggerboard strap. Yank the daggerboard out of the daggerboard well and shake the strap down over your wrist. Then stand again, placing your front foot about 5 centimetres to the windward side of the mast with the toe at the front of the mast step or, for a greater purchase on the board, up to 30 centimetres in front of the mast step. Your back foot is about 10 centimetres to the leeward side and 10 centimetres aft of the daggerboard trunk.

5 Pull the sail way over to windward with your front hand and quickly grab the boom with the back hand nearly a metre behind the forward hand. Lean your weight to windward and well aft as you sheet in.

6 Without the daggerboard, the acceleration is terrific – so be ready. If the nose starts to go to windward, besides tipping the mast forward to head off, pull the mast more to windward at the same time that you sheet out a bit (this is basically a 'shoulder roll'); then sheet in again when the mast is a little lower, and the bow will start to head downwind. After the boat starts to head off, sheeting in further will make it head off even more. Once you are moving, pull your front foot back until the toe of your front foot is a few centimetres behind the mast step.

7 If you wish to go somewhat upwind, roll the windward rail of the board underwater a bit and use the whole length of the board as a keel. But guard against stalling, because it's hard to head off from a stall. You can go 25° to 30° above a beam reach if there is enough wind, so it is sometimes possible to tack to upwind points without the daggerboard.

8 If the spout of water geysering up out of the daggerboard well gets in your eyes and annoys you, lean away from it or put your foot over it. If you go fast enough, the spouting will stop because the waterline will be behind the well.

9 If you go dead downwind, move aft to keep the nose up, pulling the mast back with you (raking it back). In a force 4 wind, your toes will be about 10 centimetres back from the daggerboard well – further aft in higher winds. Gusts are little trouble if you keep the mast raked aft, but violent gusts should be accommodated by pulling the mast hard towards you while trying to keep the centre of pressure on the sail right over the centreline of the board. Steer by banking the board like a water ski and, as usual, by raking the mast aft and to the opposite side (left if you want to go right, right if you want to go left). At the lower end of the high-wind range, say force 4, a dead downwind course in waves is often difficult. It may pay to tack downwind, crossing the waves at an angle. At force 5 and more, a dead downwind course in waves is easy as stability becomes better at higher speeds with the daggerboard out.

10 As the speed of the sailboard picks up, the bow will rise until it comes about half a metre off the water. If the board's speed picks up any more, which can happen in a force 6 wind, the bow goes back down (you can move forward a little to help it), and the board will skim along on a film of air underneath, really smacking the larger waves and becoming totally airborne now and then. Hang on tight. When you are airborne, don't

let the mast go forwards or you'll lose the sail to leeward when you land. Also, when you are about to go off the top of a wave and become airborne, don't pull back too hard. This could cause your feet to lose contact with your board, and as a result when you land the board may keep going and leave you behind. If the water is choppy, I try to absorb the bumps with slightly flexed legs like a snow skier on moguls.

When you first go at these speeds, your reaction time may not be fast enough to allow you to steer round all the waves. When you stab one, the board stops quickly – but *you* don't. Fast reactions will come with practice, though, and I guarantee that you will want to practise. This high-wind windsurfing is fun!

The upwind challenge

Going downwind at nearly three-quarters the wind speed is terrific, especially when the wind is blowing at 20 knots or more. Before you do it, though, you will first have to get a bit upwind. This can be a real challenge in any wind over force 4 if you are not using an aid like the 'Hawaii harness' or a high-wind sail. (These devices are described in Chapter 12.)

To make going upwind easier, think hard about your course and plan it so it will help you, just as you would plan a course to help you when racing. For example, it might pay to make short tacks in the lee of an island where the wind is slightly weaker; or, if there is an upwind current, to drop your sail when you want to take a break in a location where the current is strongest (something I do quite often in San Francisco Bay).

Why does a big wind tire you out so fast? Why doesn't it make you move more quickly upwind as it does downwind? The answer is aerodynamic 'drag'. Aerodynamic drag is directed downwind, opposite the direction you are now trying to travel. Much of the aerodynamic drag that affects a sailboard results from the bend of the craft's unstayed mast. As the mast bends off to leeward, the 'pocket' goes out of the sail at the top until, in a force 6 wind, the top 2 metres of sail are waving and rippling like a flag – and doing nothing but slowing you down (note the mast bend in Figure 60). The 'high-wind' sails are one solution to this problem, as they are constructed without that area at the top of a full sail which becomes flag-like. Since nearly the same area is available to

Figure 60: *Feet and hands are placed well aft when sailing in strong wind. Note the mast bend*

do the pulling, and since the drag on the little sail is less, the small sail will go faster upwind and on a reach in a strong wind. Downwind, the big sail is better since it will create a greater boat speed. Mast bend and drag will exist, but in this situation the aerodynamic drag will be directed down the line of your course, so the more aerodynamic drag the better.

Before you start out in that big wind, tighten the outhaul and downhaul to flatten the sail. The flatter you can get the sail, the less drag it will create and the less power the sail will have. In a high wind you commonly have a surplus of power.

While sailing, try to use gravity to offset the drag on the sail by tipping the mast way down to weather (the windward side of the board), the booms slanted slightly up at the back. This will help you hold the sail in position with less effort. The mast bend will cause the pocket to disappear near the mast so the front part of the sail won't be producing thrust. But the back part of the sail, which will still be correctly taut and inflated, should be kept centred and forward. The whole sail will have to be kept further forwards than usual. To provide a greater pressure on the bow to keep you from heading up during gusts, you will probably find that you will have to brace your front foot pretty far forwards.

In order to get the mast really far to weather, you have to grab the boom way back with the forward hand, 30 to 40 centimetres back of the mast. The rear hand is $\frac{1}{4}$ metre behind the front hand and is located near the centre of pressure of the sail, so most of the pull is on your rear arm. Both arms should be kept perfectly straight so that your biceps and other muscles will not have so much work to do. If the wind is not steady, you should sail about $5°$ off the highest you could point. When a lifting gust hits, you suddenly get load on your forward arm, which normally has nearly no load.

When a header gust hits, you can pull your rear arm in, flexing your biceps, to restore lift – but you won't be able to do that very often. Your arms just are not strong enough. It is better to keep the back arm straight and twist the rear shoulder away to do the sheeting. This spreads the workload to your back, which is bigger and stronger than your biceps and can do this more often.

Waves

You may never look for calm water again, except to teach a friend, after you have tried windsurfing on waves. Waves have power – power to make the windsurfing experience more thrilling, power to make you go faster and perhaps help you win a race.

Waves make water three-dimensional, turning the surface into an intriguing landscape of canyons and clefts, of hills and mountains, all turning and changing incredibly. Surfing or windsurfing is more fun than swimming, more fun than water skiing or sailing or any other water sport, because of the way you can use the waves. The first waves you sail on should be fairly regular and should not be too big, choppy or steep-fronted. Deep water swells about one metre high are best. Don't try to attack waves that drop directly onto a beach. A good place to start is inside a protected harbour which opens out into the area with waves. Then, when you get tired of falling from your board while sailing in the waves, you can duck back inside the harbour for an ego-boosting sail on flat water.

When the waves are big and the wind is light, which can happen on occasion (say, in the evening when the wind drops), windsurfing is no fun. You just stand there and get pitched around – and off. If there were powerboats on your beginner's pond, you probably found this out early. Light wind is even worse in combination with breaking beach waves. Don't go out in waves if the wind is light

a   b   c

– at least not on the sea.

Be careful going out through surf. When you first try it, the waves should be no higher than one metre (peak to trough). Find a beach where the 'break line' (the zone where most of the waves break) is a fairly distinct line parallel to shore rather than a series of separate lines behind one another out towards the sea. This kind of distinct line means that the bottom slopes fairly rapidly and will soon give you deep water in which to sail. Carry your sail out, assembled, as far as you can and then try to heave it over the break line. Paddle out to the sail quickly, put board and sail together fast, and get away before the next wave comes (see Figure 61).

Before you attempt going out, however, you should consider whether you feel really ready for the bigger problem of coming back in. If you have a really strong wind, blowing either alongshore or onshore, you can try to sail back in to the beach. If the wind isn't too strong or is offshore, stop just outside the break line, take your sail off, disconnect the outhaul and paddle in. This is necessary because, when a rigged sail gets caught in a breaking wave, the forces on the mast and booms can easily break them. Battens get broken regularly in beach waves so you might as well leave them ashore until you are fairly skilful.

Going upwind through waves is not

Figure 61 a–c: The Hawaiian beach-launch technique. The board with mast attached, is pushed out until there is enough depth for the skeg to clear. The sailor leaps aboard from the back and immediately begins sailing without the daggerboard until outside the line of breakers, at which point the daggerboard is inserted

very difficult as you have the sail to pull against and this enables you to 'power through' (see Figure 62a, b and c). If the waves are very steep, they check your forward motion a bit each time you hit one. When racing, it sometimes pays to head off a little before the next wave strikes so as to plane up over it on a diagonal.

The key to windsurfing downwind in waves is to keep your board constantly planing, for stability, speed, control, and – let's face it – fun.

If there is a lot of wind there is no problem. Point the sailboard wherever you want and *go*. The only detail to remember is to lean onto your back leg to keep the bow up, especially when you are about to start up the back of a wave.

In a weaker wind, travelling in the same direction as the waves takes much more concentration. It's often best to angle through them rather than go straight with them. This 'tacking downwind' will also help keep the sailboard planing because, when the craft

59

Figure 62: *You can sail into big waves only if you have enough wind to lean back hard against the sail as you hit each wave in order to 'power through'*

is not travelling straight with the wind, less of the boat speed is subtracted from the wind speed and the wind will provide more push. This also means there is more force in the sail to help you maintain your balance. And, of course, you can also keep your balance easier while in the crossboard stance used while reaching, because of the bracing you get from the daggerboard. Even though you may not be headed straight towards your destination, you will probably get there quicker because you are less apt to fall.

There is a unique sort of fall that commonly happens when going directly downwind in moderate or light wind in waves. You are cruising along, not any too steadily but still doing all right. Suddenly, just after you have pumped the sail once to steady a momentary imbalance, you find the sail is being blown towards you, 'backwinded' (inflated from the wrong side), from the side. It lightly hits you and into the water you go. This fall puzzled me for a long time, but after I worked out what caused it I found a way to prevent it. What happens is that, when you sheet the sail to steady yourself, you also give the board a little kick of speed and momentarily you go faster than the wind, surfing on a wave perhaps. Because there is now no pull on your arm by the sail, you tend to leave your arm pulled in after the sheeting motion so the leech edge will be pointing very close to a straight upwind direction. Since you are going faster than the wind, the slight apparent headwind and the momentum of the cloth combined tends to fold the leech over towards you behind your back. Just about now, the little burst of speed you had peters out, or you hit the next wave in front and you stop. Suddenly the wind is blowing on the wrong side of the leech, so the sail heads toward your back. The cure is simple. After every pump, carefully and gently push the sail back out and forwards again; don't continue to hold it beside yourself.

As you slide down a wave face, lean

forward a little to build up speed; then, as the next wave approaches, turn the board slightly to hit the next wave obliquely and lean your weight back to prevent the bow from submarining. Don't be timid about moving forwards and back on the board radically and often.

Currents

A current can help, or a current can hinder; what you know about them makes the difference. The first thing you have to know about currents is whether you are sailing in one. Whenever you sail, especially in a new area, check for current occasionally by performing the following simple test. Drop your sail in the water and look to the shore to find two objects which line up, one behind the other. One object should be near and the other far away. If the two objects stay aligned or move very slowly relative to one another, there is no current flowing at right angles to the line between the two objects and yourself. If the two objects do not stay in line, you are in a current.

Currents can be produced by wind but are most commonly due to river outflow or tides. River outflow creates a current that will fairly regularly move one way, whereas currents produced by tides will change direction every six hours.

When you plan a course in currents that are either constant in one direction or not liable to change soon, always choose to sail upcurrent. Even sailing straight out – not going either up or down current – can be risky. I once met a sailboarder who lost his wind at a river mouth – he had to abandon his sail to paddle in against a persistent flow that was trying to take him out into the open sea.

If the wind is at right angles to the current or is blowing opposite to the current's direction, don't sail unless you have wind about twice the speed of the current; otherwise you won't be able to make it back to where you started. If the wind and current are both in the same direction, don't sail at all if the current is more than 5 knots. If the current is less than 5 knots, sail only if the wind is about *three times* the speed of the current.

Keep watching the shoreline while sailing to check on your 'over-the-bottom' speed. In a current you can be moving at terrific speed over the water and still be going backwards!

Where I usually sail, in San Francisco Bay, the sailboarders use the strong tidal currents to help them get around. Current tables, giving the times the currents change direction as well as their speeds, are available in local boat shops. Armed with one of these tables, a sailboarder can plan ahead for a day trip using favourable currents going both east and west. We schedule many of our major round-trip endurance races to take advantage of changes in current that we know will occur during the races.

Chapter Seven
Racing

A lone sailboard sailor can certainly enjoy the experience. Tricks, exploration, the thrill of sheer speed – all can hold the interest for a long while. For most owners these activities are enough to satisfy them. Perhaps only 20 per cent of all sailboards are ever raced.

But there are reasons why every sailboard owner should come out to race on occasion. The first reason is that you may never otherwise get the chance to see boards sailed by the best sailors around. To me this is a very important reason. A race-orientated owner will be able to get more and more performance from the sailboard, for pleasure sailing as well as for racing.

Another reason to race is the chess-like quality of all sailing-boat and sailboard racing. If this intrigues you as much as it does me, you will *have* to try it. Racing sailing boats is not just a game of agility, but one of wits too, calling for continual decision-making. On a sailboard, racing has the additional appeal of making judgements about your own strength and dexterity. When all is put together, racing is very engrossing, with mind and body completely involved in the challenge.

When all sailors racing against one another have similar board- or boat-handling ability, and their equipment and physical weight are

similar, the decisive factor – the one that separates the first finishers from the last – is tactics.

This chapter will give you the basics of racing, the information that will help you close the gap between the back of the pack and the front finishers. To help you attain the number one spot, though, I strongly recommend reading additional good books that deal with yacht racing (some are listed in the bibliography).

Weight

If the sailboard is your 'yacht' and you have decided to become a top-notch racer with it, there is one thing that you must accept that will influence your tactical decisions. From the beginning, you must accept the hard fact that, if you weigh more than 70 kilograms (about 150 pounds), you can probably never be an overall world champion. This craft favours the lightweight. In fact, if you sail against someone who is just 9 kilograms (20 pounds) lighter than you and possesses equal boat-handling ability, that person can beat you to windward if you stay on the same tacks. However, if you weigh around 80 kilograms (about 180 pounds) as I do (or more), don't lose heart. You can still be placed at the front of the local fleet on occasion; you will simply have to work at it a little harder and be a bit wilier.

Major regattas such as the National Championships and the World Championships are raced in weight divisions. Starting with the 1977 World Championships, no overall world champion was sought. Rather, world

Figure 63 (opposite): *Forty sailboards started in the 1976 San Francisco Bay Crossing. Twenty made the complete round trip*

titles are now determined for each of four weight groups. These divisions, however, won't help you until you do actually compete in those high-level races. When you sail locally, you will probably be up against people 12 to 45 kilograms (about 25 to 100 pounds) lighter than you (if you are a heavyweight), and you will have to use every trick to gain a good position. If you are a lightweight, you may have been happily thinking in the past few sentences that you are on your way to fame and glory – indeed you are, potentially. In local racing you will probably be placed high by virtue of sheer good board speed; *but*, when you arrive at a National Qualifier or World Championship, your task will be even greater than that of the heavyweights. There you will find that the selection process at the lower-division level tends to bring in great numbers of lightweight sailors – many more than in the heavier weight groups. That means you'll have a lot of fine lightweight entrants to beat.

In my opinion the tendency of the sailboard to be faster under the feet of a lighter person is a good thing. This tendency is opposite to that which holds true for all small sailing boats. In small-boat classes, except when sailing in the lightest winds, the sailors often don extra clothes, soaked with water, in order to add weight when going out to race. The extra weight helps them balance their boats. In contrast, competitive sailboarders are often dieting, which is probably healthy behaviour for many members of our affluent Western society!

The best weight for a sailboarder appears to be between 50 and 65 kilograms (about 110 to 140 pounds). Bruce Matlack, three times a US National Champion, did all his winning at a weight of 59 kilograms (130 pounds). Matt Schweitzer was World Champion once at 52 kilograms (115 pounds) and again at 61 kilograms (135 pounds) when, in one year of growth from age fourteen

to fifteen, he put on 9 kilograms (20 pounds). Robbie Naish took second place in the 1976 North American Championships and first in the 1976 World Championships at a weight of 41 kilograms (90 pounds). However, a certain percentage of Robbie's success was due to the light winds in which the 1976 races were held.

In windsurfing, bigger people generally tend to do better in stronger winds. A German study indicated that force 4 (15 knots) was the turning point: lighter people finished high if the winds were less, heavier people finished in the top slots if the winds were greater. This relationship doesn't hold true with the world's very best, however. In 1975, Mike Waltze at 50 kilograms (110 pounds) beat the entire field at Marseilles in one race in a force 6 wind, and Matt Schweitzer at 61 kilograms (135 pounds) was the overall winner of the entire series, which was sailed in generally stiff winds.

There is one bright spot for the heavyweight sailor, however; weight is not a disadvantage in *extremely* light wind. This is because, as the craft's speed approaches zero, the frictional resistance of the water against the board becomes zero also – because it is proportional to the square of the speed. All you need is lots of patience for those conditions, as sailing at speeds near zero is boring.

Conditioning

The very best racers are also very strong, no matter what their weight – and that brings us to the subject of training. The muscles used in racing most small boats are primarily the stomach and leg muscles, which are placed under stress whenever the wind lightens and the sailor sits up quickly to balance the boat. These muscles are not singularly important in windsurfing. In gusty winds, where the sailboarder must make many changes in position, nearly every muscle in the body is active. In steadier winds there are only two places where there is a tendency to strain and fatigue: in the fingers, as a result of the steady tight grip, and in the forearms. Any specialized exercises for these muscles will certainly help. I have heard of people using rubber balls (which they squeeze), spring hand-exercisers, and chest-high mounted bars which they lean back against while watching TV! For me the most entertaining exercise is sailing the board itself, preferably in winds greater than force 4. Before major races, I try to sail a couple of hours every other day for a total of about four sessions. I'm careful not to sail too much on the day before the race, though, or to overdo it on the day prior to that.

Racing tactics

When you first race your sailboard, you will probably fare very poorly, but you must not let that discourage you. The first and most fundamental tactic is: gain experience. Enter every regatta that you can. Don't give up. If you find the local competition too stiff, lobby to create a strong 'B' fleet in your local area – then come to its races to support it. Or travel to compete with less experienced fleets in remote places, where it is easier to get yourself an ego-boosting win now and then.

Once you have entered a regatta, try to start every race in the regatta's series. Once in a race, try to finish it, *unless you feel that you will get too tired to start the next race* in the series. In that case you should accept that you 'Did Not Finish' (DNF is what the score sheet will say), but be sure to make the next race's start. Starts are the hardest part of any boat race, and the more that you attempt, the better for your skill. Also you will, by using this tactic, beat all the people who 'Did Not Start' (DNS) the later races of the day (usually about a quarter of the fleet), because you get one point sub-tracted from your score for each boat that does not start when you do.

Whenever you are tempted to give up because the wind has become very weak, you must remind yourself that the score sheet will only show how people in the race finished – not what they endured! Besides, you will never gain the skill to sail well in light winds if you don't attempt to race in them when you have the chance.

The cardinal rules for racing

1 Enter the races.
2 Finish the races.
3 Don't fall!
4 Don't drop your sail unless by not doing so you risk violating rule 3.

With respect to rules 3 and 4, if an opponent threatens to pass you and you feel that in trying to hold him off you will take a chance of going beyond your boat-handling ability and have a fall, let him pass! If you fall or drop your sail, you may be passed by many others.

The foregoing tactical principles are oriented primarily towards people who race sailboards. Almost all other tactical rules developed for racing sailing boats will work for windsurfing races as well. The following discussion pertains to those sailing-boat racing tactics that are the most helpful to sailboard racers.

Your 'weapons'

There are three 'weapons' that you can use to win your races. The first is *good board speed* – a quality dependent on general board handling, your weight and your physical condition. The second weapon is your *physical presence* on the course when you encounter an opponent. (When you have right of way by the sailing 'rules-of-the-road', your opponent must make a turn to avoid you or risk being disqualified for touching you.) The third weapon is your *blanketing cone*, the zone of disturbed air that your sail leaves behind.

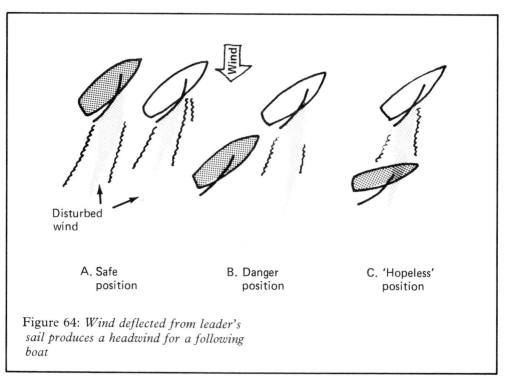

A. Safe position   B. Danger position   C. 'Hopeless' position

Disturbed wind

Figure 64: *Wind deflected from leader's sail produces a headwind for a following boat*

In Figure 64(a), two sailboards are going upwind with the white craft leading. The blanketing cones are marked with shaded triangles. In this case both boards have 'clear air' and will proceed to windward equally well if both are sailed equally well. In Figure 64(b), the white board is directly ahead of the black board. The sailor with the black craft will find that that board will not point as high as the white board without stalling because it is feeling a headwind produced by the wind deflected from the leader's sail. Generally, if you can look forward and see the leech of your upwind opponent's sail directly in line with his or her mast, you are thoroughly in a blanketing cone, and will be driven downwind rapidly in the next few seconds as you try to keep from stalling. Your two craft will soon acquire the positions shown in Figure 64(c), and will stay in that relationship with the gap between them gradually opening to 10 to

20 metres, at which point the blanketing effect is no longer very great. When you are racing you must constantly be aware not only of the times that you are in someone's blanketing cone, but also of the times when, by not carefully avoiding the situation, you are about to sail into someone's blanketing cone. Similarly, the blanketing cone is a weapon you can use to keep opponents from passing you and, when you are going downwind, one that you can use to pass them.

A first race

Sailboard racing is usually conducted by the Windsurfer Class Association, or sailboard associations, in conjunction with a local yacht club. Races take place over what is known as a Port Hand Olympic Triangle Course. Details concerning the course, and various other sailing instructions, are issued by the organizing club on receipt of your entry.

The format for a windsurfing regatta is fairly standard. After you have completed your entry form, full details of the racing, start times, venue, directions thereto, and insurance and buoyancy requirements are issued. After that, simply turn up at the regatta site in good time with your sailboard. A skippers' meeting takes place at which all the participants are briefed about any special requirements or positions of the course. This generally includes weather forecast, tidal variations and any local hazards such as rocks or strong currents. If you have any questions or doubts, now is the time to ask the organizers. Don't be shy; there are probably half a dozen others just as anxious as you are, but not wanting to make themselves conspicuous by asking what they may consider to be silly questions.

This meeting over, the next item on your agenda must be to prepare your board for the first race, check that the mast step fits tight, and that the daggerboard is just tight enough to stay down but can easily be lifted out by its strap.

Sail out to the area of the start and look around to establish the wind speed. Set the outhaul and downhaul according to your estimation, but make allowances for the length of the course and how much upwind sailing there will be. Set your outhaul tighter for a long course or one that will need much beating. After your outhaul has been set, be sure to tuck the free end of the line around the boom and underneath itself to help secure it. The middle of a race is no place to have an outhaul come free!

At about ten minutes before start time, sail upwind to check the wind's range of shiftiness. Stay on one tack. If you get a header (an adverse wind shift), make a mental note of what object your board's nose is pointing to onshore, but keep on your course until you get a lift (a favourable wind shift), then tack over and make a mental note of the shoreside

object towards which you are now pointing. Remember the two places that you noted; they are your tacking marks. During the race, whenever you find your board pointing at one of them, it is time to change tack (assuming the *average* wind direction does not change). Also make note of how often the wind is shifting; if it is shifting very rapidly, it often doesn't pay to tack on headers.

At about five minutes to race time, get back to the starting line to see if one end of it has an advantage over the other. Sail right up to the centre of the line and park your sailboard with the nose pointing at the buoy at one end of the line, and the tail pointing at the buoy at the other. Hold the sail by the uphaul only, with the mast vertical, and look carefully at the position of the clew of the sail relative to your board. Sail to the end of the line furthest from the clew of your sail. That end is the most advantageous end of the start line. If the difference between the two ends isn't very great, stay at the centre.

Starting

I will list here only two of the ways you can get a good start; there are several others (see Figure 65).

'Hunt and peck' is what Dick Lamb, the 1976–77 North American Windsurfer Association president, calls the most popular starting technique. Dick is good at it, but then he is good at all kinds of starting techniques and rarely loses a start. 'Hunt and peck' is very straightforward but takes a bit of bravado to do well. You search around looking for an open spot between the other boards into which you can poke your board. At about thirty seconds to go, try to sail in close to the starboard buoy but stay a couple of board lengths downwind of the starting line. Try, by whatever legal means available, to keep a little open water to leeward – *especially* try to avoid letting that spot be occupied by someone lighter than you or by someone you know

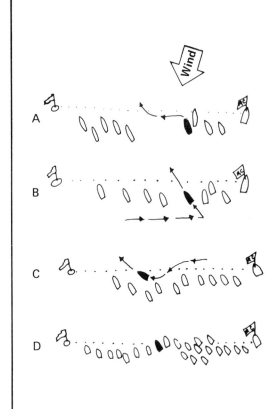

A pictorial summary of starting techniques

A. 'Hunt and Pack'
Luff up sailboards crowding you to windward; keep clear water to leeward

B. 'Port tack approach'
Cross over a hole in the line and tack over to starboard to shoot through it right at the start

C. 'Dip start'
Sail down into a hole from the windward side of the line just before the start; then head up and recross the line. (One-minute rule forbids this when it is in effect)

D. 'Aggressive fleet'
Hide behind the sails of your over-eager competitors. If they get called 'over early' and you don't, your gamble will work

Figure 65

is a better sailor. At about fifteen seconds to go, you should begin to accelerate. Bear off into your leeward open space if you are early at the line. At the gun, turn up across the line. When you are getting into your spot don't let anyone pass you to windward. Head them up across the starting line if they try to get slightly ahead of you prior to the start. Of course, be careful not to go across the line yourself.

For those with a less aggressive style a good approach is to go down to the port end and, at about thirty seconds to go, start sailing parallel to and a bit behind the starting line toward the starboard end. (This is assuming the port end is *not* the favourable end, because in that

case you will probably have to use 'hunt and peck' with you and your competitors on port tack.) Most of the other boats will be heading up towards the line as they 'hunt and peck', so you will have to sail below their sterns. Somewhere on the starting line there is likely to be a gap between the starboard tack boats. Sail past this hole, then tack over onto starboard at about ten seconds to go and head up toward the line at full speed. This technique will usually work, but every so often you will not find a hole prior to the start. Should that happen, don't go onto starboard for the start but try to break through the line on port, right after the start. It is rare that you will have to go below more than one or

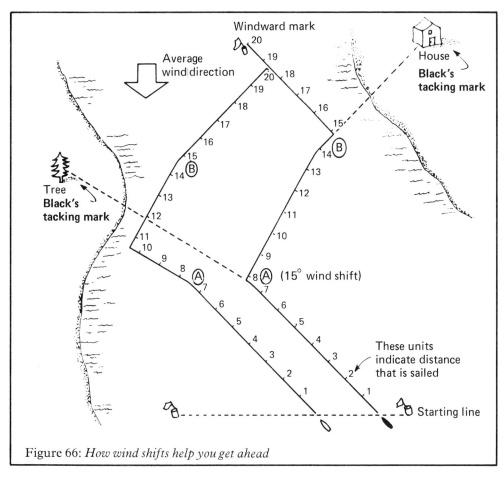

Figure 66: *How wind shifts help you get ahead*

two of your opponents when doing this, and it is better to do that than to tack over into someone's blanketing cone.

Wind shifts

Now you are on your way upwind to the first mark. This leg of the course is often decisive. You must bring all your concentration to bear on gaining clear wind and keeping it, and ever, ever following the shifts in the wind. Go high. Try to go higher. When going as high as it will go, a sailboard feels as if it is going sideways, and to a certain extent it is. The nose will point about 10° to windward of the direction you are actually going. Again, keep following the wind shifts. Doing the right thing when

shifts occur can gain more distance for you than anything else you can do.

Figure 66 shows why wind shifts can help so much. The black and the white boards both get a good start and are even until the headwind hits them both at A. The black sailboard tacks but the white one does not. White finally tacks, but at B another shift brings the wind back to where it was at the start. Again black tacks but white does not. The black sailboard beats white to the mark because, as seen in the figure, it has sailed a shorter distance than the opposition.

To find the shifts, you use the two tacking marks that you memorized prior to the start of the race. Good marks are

69

very far away so that parallax as you advance past them is not significant. It takes practice to follow wind shifts correctly, so practise following them even when you are out sailing for fun. Then during a race, the technique will help you get where you want to go faster.

The upwind course

To get back to the race: shortly after the start, you must decide which tack is the lifted one and get onto it. Except for following the wind shifts, try to obey the upwind rule: sail the longest tacks first. When you are up nearer to the mark, you will make shorter tacks to avoid errors in estimation that could cause you to 'overstand the mark' (to sail more upwind than you need to).

If you keep ahead, well and good; but, if you are behind, you will start encountering your competitors on opposite tacks. When your right hand is in front, you have right-of-way. When on this tack (starboard), you should hail competitors on a collision course with you. Shout out 'starboard!' decisively; it tends to keep people from trying to squeak past your bow.

Suppose you are on a port tack which you think is lifted, and you encounter an opponent on starboard on a collision course. In general, you should not tack to avoid your opponent, but should go below your opponent's stern. The 2 to 3 metres you lose here will be more than made up by the lift you are on.

If you must tack for an opponent, try to do it early; don't let other sailors get you into their blanketing cones.

Rounding the marks

When rounding marks you must concentrate, because you can gain or lose a lot of places at marks. The best tactic at weather marks (those most upwind) is to be conservative and careful not to fall or to pass too close to the mark. If you touch the mark you must go around it

again in the original direction – in other words, a complete circle. Falls at marks are the worst kind you can have, because everyone else piles up on you, making it rather difficult to get started again.

The reaching course

As you round the weather mark, watch out for a closely following competitor. If someone is right behind you, head off onto the reach gradually to keep your opponent from going upwind of you and blanketing you. If you are the following boat, try at first to go upwind of your competitor. If your opponent won't let you go by, try to turn downwind quickly and dive through his or her lee. The element of surprise is on your side if you do this fast enough. If nobody is close behind or ahead, head off quickly and get your board planing on the reach as soon as you can.

If the wind is fairly strong, you should estimate before rounding the weather mark whether you will be able to sail the reach with your daggerboard in, or if you will have to take it out. If the latter is necessary, I usually sail off on a beam reach after rounding the mark in order to get out of the way of people rounding behind me. Then I stop, pull out my daggerboard, and head off downwind on the broad reach. What you *don't* want to do is decide halfway down the reach that you want to take your daggerboard out. Try your hardest to estimate correctly; it may cost you a fall if you misjudge.

On the reaching leg, the sailing philosophy of 'down in the gusts, up in the lulls' applies. The key is to keep your board planing as much as you can. Going slightly downwind in the gusts tends to help you do that; you will stay in the gust for a slightly longer time since you will be moving in its direction. Going upwind in the lulls is especially important if by not doing so you lose your plane. It takes more wind to break free and *start* planing than to *keep* planing, so be more concerned with keeping on a plane than with keeping on your course to the next mark.

Work the waves. Except in light winds, waves move more slowly than you do; that means you will be coming up the backs of the waves and then going down their fronts. Find the low places in the waves to go through, running along the front of the wave you just came down until you find the weak spot in the one just ahead. Rock forward as you come down the front of a wave and lean back as you come to the bottom.

As much as you can, without allowing upwind competitors a chance to blanket you, try for the inside line on the reaches. This gives you right-of-way at the marks and allows you to come up from below on your opposition at the gybe mark.

Do not cut the gybe mark too close on the approach side or you will swing wide on the far side and leave room for someone to cut inside and blanket you (see Figure 67). This goes for the leeward mark too. The gybe and leeward marks are the easiest places for you to pass an opponent you have been following. Watch carefully – if your opponent goes wide on the far side, sneak inside on the exit side and blanket him or her!

If I approach a leeward mark with my daggerboard out, I will sometimes try to insert it while still moving by sailing a bit low of the mark before rounding, then dropping it in and heading up around the mark. This is a tricky manoeuvre, however, and I don't often risk it. If I choose not to risk it, I sail past the mark with the daggerboard still out, then lower my sail a bit to stabilize the board and re-insert the daggerboard.

The downwind course

Downwind legs are the toughest. Don't fall. Be conservative. If you must, reach off instead of run – you'll get there quicker if you don't fall. In a very heavy

Figure 67: *Both these windsurfing sailors are leaving too much room on the exit side of this gybe mark. 26320 especially should have begun his gybe earlier so as to be able to pass upwind of 26345 just below the mark*

wind, luffing downwind can actually pay off since you may regain some strength to use on the next beat. If the wind is light, don't pull out your daggerboard. Leaving the daggerboard in seems to make no perceptible difference in board speed when the wind is light, and the stability and steering you lose by removing it may provoke a fall.

In general, it is a bad practice to blanket your competitors very closely on downwind legs. If they fall in front of you while you are doing it, you will almost certainly collide with them. When someone tries to blanket me I sometimes start veering and rocking; that makes the following sailor worry – sometimes with good reason!

When going from a run to a beat around the leeward mark, again be careful to go wide on the approach side and tight on the exit. Often you can't steer too well when doing this turn since you are heavily blanketed by opponents behind you, so round the mark very cautiously and somewhat slowly. Don't be flashy; work the sail carefully and gently. Don't sheet in quickly. If

somebody behind you blankets you as you pull in fast, you may wind up sitting on the mark instead of rounding it.

Finishing

If your finish is upwind, one end of the finish line may have advantages over the other. The favourable end of a finish line is the most downwind end (see Figure 68). (This contrasts with the favourable end of a starting line, which is the most upwind end.) As you approach the line, try to estimate which end this is – not easy but, if you don't you could well be beaten by someone who is actually behind you.

Other tactics

When sailing a very long race or one in very heavy wind, you should change your tactics somewhat. Be more conservative at the start and definitely don't risk any false starts. In a long race the start becomes much less important. Also, plan your energy expenditure. Don't shoot all your bolts at once. Spread your strength out around the course. The sailor who surges ahead of you may not be able

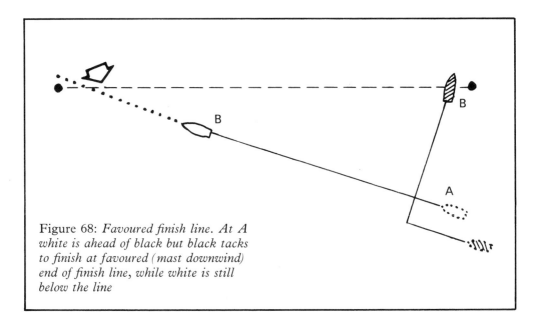

Figure 68: *Favoured finish line. At A white is ahead of black but black tacks to finish at favoured (mast downwind) end of finish line, while white is still below the line*

to keep it up. Sometimes it even pays to look for places where the wind may be weaker since a really strong wind makes the full-size windsurfing sail less efficient. In any event, avoid areas where the wind is gusty, such as the middle of the back of the pack, since gusts can tire you far faster.

In very light winds you will get the best board speed if you lean your sail somewhat to leeward, the way a beginner often does. This will cause the cloth to hang in a better aerofoil shape than if the sail were straight up. Also remember that, by Rule 60 of the International Yatch Racing Union (IYRU) rules under which we race, pumping your sail is usually forbidden. This rule is more often infringed than any other, and with good reason – pumping definitely helps move you through the water in light winds.

One last aspect of racing tactics warrants mention. It has to do with knowing the nature of your competitors and how your decisions should be influenced by their behaviour as individuals with different personalities. I

Figure 69: *If the wind is not too gusty, the upwind course can be sailed with an arm hooked inside the boom. Besides conserving energy, this technique is valuable because it brings the mast further over the windward side of the board*

have observed that a truly competitive sailor who is very good can match any manoeuvre you do and beat you! With this in mind, it is sometimes wise to stay out of sight of anyone faster than you whom you have managed to pass. Also watch out for 'sea lawyers', especially in light-wind racing. These people try to intimidate their competitors by shouting rules at them. Sometimes these people are right, though, so your best defence is to know the yacht-racing rules thoroughly yourself. Get an RYA rulebook and learn as much as you can. That completes the basics. A bit of practice will help, and so will additional reading. Check the bibliography for a few of the best titles I know. May your mantel collapse under the weight of all your trophies.

Chapter Eight
Games and Freestyle

Not everybody likes to race. Some people consider racing too controlled. Some don't like the 'I win, you lose' nature of all racing. For these windsurfing people there are fleet activities with challenges quite different from racing which offer a real diversion for even the most skilled sailboard sailor.

Freestyle

Freestyle has recently become a recognized competitive event with panels of judges scoring participants' tricks done in a three-minute interval, but of course it can be done outside a competition, alone, simply to impress onlookers.

The varieties of tricks are limited only by the sailor's imagination, but here are the best-known tricks.

Figure 70 (opposite)

Figure 72 (below): *Derk Thijs of Holland, European champion in 1973, 1974 and 1975, does a body dip from a Windglider*

1 *Variations on straight sailing:*
  (a) with back to sail
  (b) on lee side of sail
  (c) on lee side with back to sail
  (d) inside booms
  (e) inside booms with back to sail
  (f) stern first
  (g) kneeling
  (h) sitting
  (i) lying down
2 *Spins*: These involve alternately tacking and gybing as fast as possible. Try for the maximum number of spins in the shortest time.
3 *Spin tacking*: Tacking by going around face forwards.
4 *Head dip*: Sheet out, bend your head over backwards and drag it underwater. Sheet in again to come back up.
5 *Bottom dip*: Drag your bottom in the water.
6 *Body dip:* Sheet out, drag your body underwater with head left dry. Sheet in and come up.

Figure 73: *Ken Winner of Maryland comes up from a very difficult head dip, done while sailing with back to sail*

7 *Nose dip*: Stand with back to sail. Sheet out, bending knees until your face touches the water, then sheet in to come back up. (Few and far between are those who can do this trick!)

8 *Water start*: In shallow water get under the sail, which lies to windward of the board. Place your feet on the board and push up on the booms to lift the sail into the wind. Hope for a gust strong enough to pick you up and deposit you on the board. (Grabbing the mast with the forward hand near the universal allows this to be done in less wind.)

9 *Nose sink/tail sink*: On a run, step back until the nose of the board stands up at a 45° angle. Done quickly, this trick is called a 'wheelie'. Or take out the daggerboard and stand on the nose with the skeg forward and up out of the water.

10 *Lee-side tacks*: Make a series of tacks upwind, staying on the same side of the board. On alternate tacks you will be sailing normally; on the other tacks you will be on the lee side of the sail.

11 *Submarining*: Walk towards the nose while continuing to sheet in, driving the board underwater. See how deep you can go before the board squirts backwards.

12 *Rail riding*: Hook your forward foot under the windward rail and pull up until you can rest the shin of your forward leg on the rail. You can sail that way, or, if your're really hot, you can step up with both feet on the rail.

13 *Flip*: For a finale you can do an over-the-boom flip into your sail, trying not to land on your battens. Then jump to your feet and run back to your board before the sail sinks beneath you.

If there are two or more of you, try stunts like standing with one foot on each board or standing on each other's shoulders. Or, one person can sail while the other does headstands on the board. For a real challenge, get one person to sail while the other stands and tosses a Frisbee back and forth to another windsurfer.

Figure 71: *The head dip is the first trick a windsurfing sailor learns*

a.

b.

c.

d.

Figure 74 a–d (opposite page): *A spin tack by Ken Winner, a trick which he perfected. The sailor makes a 540° turn on the board while changing from one tack to the other*

Figure 75 (above): *Ken Winner demonstrates the first two stages of the pirouette turn while sailing on a reach. The sailor performs a 360° turn in place. The key to this trick is carefully tipping the sail to windward and then luffing it in a balanced position*

Figure 76 (top): *A stern-first rail ride.
Placing one foot on the daggerboard helps
enable the sailor to gain a standing positic
as in Figure 78*

Figure 77: (above): *Lee-side rail ride*

Figure 78: (left): *A standing rail ride insi
the booms*

Figure 79 a–f (opposite page): *'The
helicopter'. The clew of the sail is pushed
leeward and then around the front of the
board*

Slalom races

In slalom racing, the boats are started in pairs and race against each other in a series of heats. As in regular racing, this kind of competition is often won by the sailboarder who best obeys these two rules: *stay dry* and *don't drop your sail*.

The course is raced first upwind and then downwind. In such a course, illustrated in Figure 82, contestants are required to make very tight turns on occasion, and they are also required to cross each other's course en route to the finish.

One of the great virtues of the course is that it is easily constructed, using only six buoys, about 100 metres of 8 millimetre line, four small bricks, and two anchors.

Rules for this course are as follows:

1 Buoys may be hit without penalty.
2 Intentional interference with the opponent is not allowed.
3 A boat on port tack should keep clear of a boat on starboard tack.
4 When the boats cross at the top of the course, the boat on port tack shall keep clear of the boat on starboard tack.
5 When the boats meet on one side of the course, the boat which is behind in the race shall keep clear of the boat which is ahead.

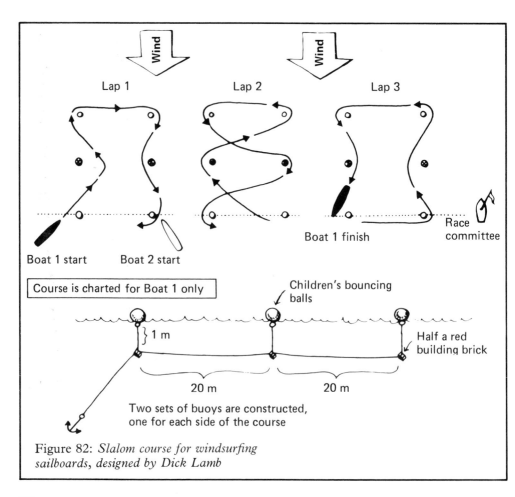

Figure 82: *Slalom course for windsurfing sailboards, designed by Dick Lamb*

Figure 80 (above): *Slalom races are exciting for both participants and spectators*

Figure 81 (right): *Competitors in slalom races may use any sail or daggerboard but otherwise their craft must be standard windsurfing sailboards*

Figure 83: *The foot drag is a braking method that is useful when sailing slalom courses in high winds*

Buoyball

Many highly skilled sailboarders won't even launch their boards to pleasure sail or race if the wind is less than force 4, but Buoyball will bring them out onto the water in near-zero wind! In fact, Buoyball is so much fun that, if the wind is blowing a steady force 5 on a day planned for Buoyball, there will be a lot of disappointed people because, though force 5 is a perfect wind for high-speed pleasure sailing it's too much for Buoyball. Buoyball provides an opportunity to enjoy sailing in light wind.

Buoyball is a team sport played on windsurfing sailboards. It is getting to be so popular that some of its adherents envision a day when giant stadiums may be built to accommodate cheering legions of spectators. The game is a bit risky since toes can get mashed and ankles

bashed, but what a riotous good time it is! Like any good team sport, the fun is well worth the bruises.

While the rules of this game are still under development, the ones listed below were in effect as of January 1980.

The court: A goal is designated by two buoys placed 5 metres apart on a line which is perpendicular to the wind direction. A third buoy, called a 'clearing buoy', is placed directly downwind of the goal, about 30 to 50 metres away. Upwind of the goal or downwind of the 'clearing buoy' are considered out of bounds. There need be no bounds set on the sides.

The ball: Use a child's bouncing ball made of vinyl. This ball has a flexible ring moulded into it which can be slipped over a wrist or ankle, leaving the hands free for sailing. The ball is inflated to a 35 centimetre diameter.

Teams: Two teams of three to six players each are chosen. For larger teams, it is wise to place the goal further from the clearing buoy.

Figure 84: *While playing Buoyball,
players are trying to get the ball upwind.
Backhanded passes are often required.*

Rules of play:

1 To put the ball into play, a member
of the team with possession must
carry the ball around the clearing
buoy and head upwind. A flip of a
coin determines which team will have
initial possession, but thereafter the
team that is scored against picks up
the ball at the goal and proceeds
downwind to the clearing buoy to put
the ball back into play.

2 A player in possession of the ball or
one attempting to pick up the ball
must have his sail up and no more
than $\frac{1}{4}$ metre of the clew end of the
rig submerged or in one-sided water
contact.

3 When the hull of an opposing player
comes in contact with the hull of the
player in possession, the ball carrier
must release the ball. The ball carrier
may not throw the ball after being
tagged, but he must drop it in place.

4 A player who has yielded the ball by
releasing it after having been tagged
by an opponent may not touch the
ball again until an interval of ten
seconds has elapsed or an opponent or
team-mate has touched the ball.

5 To score, a player must throw the
ball upwind or sail upwind so that
some part of the ball crosses the goal
line.

6 Three points are received for a
throwing score and five points are
received for sailing the ball through
the goal.

7 The ball must be dropped by the
possessor if one of his team-mates
commits a foul.

8 Any player who causes deliberate
injury, or injury because of excess
speed or a gross manoeuvring error,
to another player or to a referee, has
committed a foul and is subject to
immediate removal from the game.
That player's team must continue one
player short until a score is made, at
which time a substitution may be
made.

9 A team may make one substitution
per game.

10 The sail rig cannot be used to
impede the progress of an opponent;

such use constitutes a foul. Only *boards* may come in contact with an opponent's board. If a player loses control of his or her rig and an opponent collides with it, the sailor with the downed rig is liable for a penalty.

11 Penalties for fouls differ for offensive and defensive players. If an offensive player commits a foul, his or her team loses possession of the ball and the ball carrier must release it. A defensive player who commits a foul must sail downwind until he or she is the further player from the goal, and then complete a 720° turn before resuming play.

12 Sailing right-of-way rules generally do not apply to participants in the game except in the case where they encounter a non-participant in the playing area. However, while the ball is being returned downwind after a score preparatory to placing it again in play, sailing right-of-way rules are in effect for all participants.

13 Play proceeds until one of the two teams has scored over twenty points or until one and a half hours have passed, whichever occurs first.

Chapter Nine
Maintenance

When people without prior knowledge of windsurfing see sailboards for the first time, they usually suppose that they are constructed like surfboards. Happily, they are not. Surfboards, though beautiful, are fragile. Modern windsurfing sailboards are made of polyethylene and are extremely durable. Like another polyethylene product, the Frisbee, the board is nearly indestructible.

Polyethylene construction does have its mechanical drawbacks, though. The very features – softness and floppiness – that make polyethylene impossible to chip or fracture *also* prevent this difficult material from lying smooth and fair on the surface of your hull. Indeed, so far as I know, every sailboard hull ever made has some little ripple or dent on the bottom – and usually a few on the top too.

Those ripples and dents don't seem to make any real difference in board speed. A good sailboarder can win a race on the most dented board in the fleet, while a poorer sailboarder can lose the same race on the fairest board; it happens constantly. Nor do the dents indicate a thin spot in the hull which will cause trouble later on. The dents are there simply because the material is polyethylene, not fibreglass, a difference which will be appreciated the first time you drop your sailboard and nothing happens to it. I have twice dropped sailboards from my car roof while travelling along the highway, with no damage to the boards either time except for scratches where they first hit the asphalt.

On occasion, a polyethylene windsurfing board will need repair. The repairs are normally to correct problems which can only be labelled manufacturing defects, and are not typical problems at all. These problems occur only with specific boards.

Cracks and holes

This is the procedure for fixing a broken daggerboard well. First obtain a hot-melt (thermoplastic) glue from your local sailboard dealer and a supply of 'all-purpose glue sticks'. Also get a steel rod about $\frac{1}{2}$ centimetre in diameter. Be sure you have some gloves to wear too – hot glue gives nasty burns. If there is a large amount of water inside the board, it should be removed. This is done by first boring a 1 centimetre ($\frac{1}{2}$ inch) diameter, 5 centimetre (2 inch) deep hole into the board at the point where the water is thought to lie. The board is then hung up in rope slings with the bored hole facing downward. The corner of a square of paper towel is now shoved up into the hole with a pencil or other blunt tool. The water will flow by capillary action into the towel and out of the board. The water will evaporate from the portion of the towel that hangs in the air outside the board. Let the towels do their work until they no longer stay wet. This time interval can be anywhere from one to six weeks.

After the water has been removed, you are ready to repair the cracks and also the holes that you made in the water-removal process.

Plug in the glue gun and alow to heat

up thoroughly. For maximum heat, don't use an extension cord on the gun. Stand the board on its tail against a wall. Melt the nose of the gun through the bottom of the board about 1 centimetre behind the daggerboard well. (If the crack extends all along the back of the well, use an electric drill to bore down parallel to the crack.) Begin poking glue sticks into the gun and pump them into the board. Shove in lots of sticks, three to ten, and keep putting them in until melted glue starts to well up along the crack. Now try to cram in some unmelted glue sticks, two or three of them, to further add to the material reinforcing the back of the daggerboard well. After the glue cools, do the same to the board's top, melting or drilling through just behind the daggerboard well and pumping in more sticks until glue wells up out of the crack.

Stand the board against the wall; the end of the daggerboard well on which you are working should be down. Heat one end of the steel rod on a gas stove or with a torch until it is quite hot, just below red hot. Wearing gloves, pick up the rod and use the hot end to melt down through the glue that welled up out of the crack. Melt down until the rod melts the edges of the crack itself. Stir and puddle the glue and melted daggerboard-well material (the polyethylene) while watching out for a bulging of the daggerboard well sides near the rod. If such bulging begins, withdraw the hot rod immediately and douse the well with cold water.

Allow the glue to cool for half an hour at least. Then examine the crack to see if any bubbles have come to the surface while it was cooling, leaving holes in the melted plastic. Usually there are several bubble holes. Heat the rod again and remelt the area around the bubble holes; then, while the holes are filled, douse the

daggerboard well with icy water to chill it before the next bubble breaks the surface.

Cut excess hot-melt glue lumps from your repaired areas with a serrated kitchen knife, using liberal amounts of cold water as a lubricant to keep the knife from getting stuck to the glue.

The mast-step well can be repaired in much the same way, using the gun to melt through the deck and fill the void that has developed beside the well.

A more extreme problem is presented by a board that has insufficient polyurethane foam inside or has foam which has become crushed due to repeated impacts (usually falling students). Use a 2 centimetre ($\frac{3}{4}$ inch) hole saw to drill holes in the afflicted area. Next, use paper towels and a hair dryer for drying what moisture there may be inside. Then fill the void with two-part foam-in-place polyurethane foam.

Figure 86: *Repairing a void in the foam near a mast step well. First use a hole saw to remove some plugs of plastic to gain access. Dry any water inside with paper towels wrapped around a dowel and with a hair drier*

Figure 85 (opposite): *The heart of a sailboard, the stainless and nylon universal mechanism*

Saw off the excess with a long carpenter's saw, weld the plugs back in (the ones your hole saw cut out), and you should be back on the water within a couple of hours. Figure 86 shows a void near the step well that was causing a chronically loose mast step. The board is now alive and well and sailing happily.

The thing to remember when using the hot-melt glue gun on the skin of the sailboard is that you are actually doing a gasketing operation, not just applying glue to the crack. Pump in enough glue to fill the void behind the crack as well as the crack itself. Completely surround the lips of the crack inside and out to prevent water passage.

Bending a board

You may wish to modify your poly-ethylene board's curvature. Some boards won't sail well otherwise.

The most common change desired is the addition of 'nose' or 'scoop' to the board, making it easier to sail in large waves. A nose that tips up strongly does not tend to 'pearl' (dive underwater) as easily as one less tipped. Use heat lights to soften the skin plastic of the area where you want to make the bend. With the lights, thoroughly heat (but not to bubbling) the plastic on the bottom and the top of the board, from about $\frac{1}{2}$ metre from the nose to $\frac{1}{2}$ metre ahead of the mast. Wedge the nose under some strong stationary object and apply considerable force to the tail of the board in order to bend the nose at the heated region. Alternatively, provide supports for the nose and tail, and apply a heavy weight to the area that was heated – for example, get a couple of friends to stand on it there. While the pressure is still on, cool the hot area with a douse of cold water and the 'scoop' will stay. Putting strong scoop into a board may leave wrinkles in the skin on the board's top, but this is not a problem except in an aesthetic sense. The Hawaiians scoop their boards heavily.

These paragraphs intimate how easy it is to bend a polyethylene sailboard. Indeed, it is very easy. In fact, you have to exercise a certain amount of care with your board to prevent bending it permanently by accident. Therefore, when you store a sailboard always keep its flexibility in mind; arrange your storage supports either to reinforce the board's natural curvature or at least not to affect it in any way. The most neutral way to store boards is on edge or on end. If you store yours by hanging it from ropes from garage rafters (as many people do), place the board upside down in the ropes if they are closer together than $1\frac{1}{2}$ metres, and right side up if they are further apart than that.

The sail rig

Parts that break on the sail rig must be replaced if the sailboard is to conform to racing regulations. If this is not important to you, the broken boom or mast can often be spliced with fibreglass tape and epoxy resin.

How do you break a mast or boom? Not easily. They are very rugged despite their light weight. Sometimes a mast will break at the boom line from repeated falls (more often when one is sailing with a harness), but the most common cause is from ramming the mast or booms into the sea bottom when windsurfing in breaking waves. People who do a lot of windsurfing in breaking waves say the fun is worth the risk. Be careful in waves, though; your body is not as easy to repair as your board is.

The mast base, the dowel which slides up into the epoxy mast, was made of soft wood on the older sailboards. These parts often swell up and jam in the mast, plugging it so tightly that water trapped inside cannot get out. Likewise new water can't get in. If it is fresh water trapped in there, it will cause the mast base to rot, and within two years the mast will break off at the connection to the epoxy tube. The rot problem is one good reason to remove the mast base from the mast on occasion, and to sand it down a little each time it is taken out. There is another reason to remove and sand the base, even in salt-water areas where the mast bases rarely rot out; the base can get so tight that it will not allow the mast to make the occasional quarter-pivot that it sometimes needs to make when dropped. If the mast can't easily do this twist at the base, it will stick and leave the downhaul wrapped part way around the mast, making it hard to undo.

Hawaiian sailboarders coat the tops of their soft-wood mast bases with polyester resin, or replace them with the newer teakwood bases. The plastic universal joint is also popular in Hawaii. These units have a freer turning action because they have a second 360° swivel at the connection of the U-joint to the base, allowing the sail to turn over while in the 'down' position, which may happen when a wave or strong gust of wind hits.

The best way to remove a mast base that's stuck in a mast tube is to pound it out from the inside. To do this, get a 40 centimetre (about 1¼ foot) length of 19 millimetre (¾ inch) diameter steel rod and drop it in the hollow end at the top of the mast where the mast tip is inserted. Bounce the mast up and down a bit and the base will neatly fall out with no damage to the mast.

On occasion, in locations where the wind dies unexpectedly, sailboarders may drop masts overboard while attempting to use them as paddles (having removed the sail and booms first). Masts are expensive, so, if you have ever been tempted to remove your mast from the booms while out on the water, it is wise to have previously stuffed a chunk of expanded polyethylene or polyurethane into each end of the mast to keep water from entering.

I have also heard of several universal joints being lost overboard when beginners allowed the downhaul to come untied and then attempted to lift the sail.

Before loaning your rig to any beginner, make sure that the downhaul knots are very secure.

When a boom bumper comes off, replace it quickly. The bumper is not there to protect you from injury, as many people suppose; rather, it is there to protect the board from the sharp edges of the W-spring at the front of the booms. If you make a forward fall on a sailboard that has no boom bumper, you can cut little notches in your board, perhaps all the way through to the foam.

Usually boom bumpers come off for only one reason: the booms were put on upside down, with the uphaul coming over the top of the bumper. Be careful to lead the uphaul out of the bottom of the booms when rigging (as illustrated in Chapter 3).

Teak booms need no care; teakwood is almost totally weatherproof. If you don't want them to turn white, as they will naturally, you can keep them brown by sanding them occasionally and then rubbing them with teak oil. I don't do this though. The only care that I give my booms is to sand them across the grain with coarse sandpaper prior to going out racing. This makes the booms slip less in my hands when I get tired.

There is no class regulation against sanding booms, so many small people take advantage of this permission and sand the booms much smaller in diameter to fit their hands. Use restraint when sanding down booms, though; the booms will lose both stiffness and strength when made smaller.

People who sail much with the 'Hawaii harness' (described in Chapter 12) are well advised to replace the wood screws that attach the booms to the metal W-spring with 5 centimetre (2 inch) number 10 flathead machine screws. The screw heads should be on the inside of the booms and well countersunk to avoid chafing on the mast; the nuts will be inside the boom bumper. This 'through bolting' will reduce the chance of boom delamination.

If a boom delamination begins, you can usually stop it by pouring two-part epoxy resin or glue into the gap. The factory will usually replace badly delaminated booms.

Aluminium booms can corrode if used much in salt water; thus it is wise to rinse them with fresh water after salt-water use.

Many people use resin products on their hands rather than roughing up their booms. This is fine except that once you *start* using it, you have to *keep on* using it. Resin stays on your booms and actually makes them more slippery when you aren't using it on your hands. It also gives you the most incredible callouses you have ever seen.

Daggerboards

Wooden daggerboards get chewed up faster than any other piece of windsurfing apparatus. Fill gouges on the leading edge of the daggerboard with polyester auto-body putty. A chewed-up trailing edge is harder to deal with; you will have to re-profile it with fibreglass cloth and polyester resin. Better still, prevent the problem by being careful with your wooden daggerboard. What chews up the leading and trailing edges fastest is quick removal of the board from the well. One thing that can help your daggerboard to survive is to use a penknife to round the front and back edges of the daggerboard-well trunk on the board bottom. While you are at it, go all the way round the well to round it out – which ensures that you won't ever cut yourself when carrying the board with your hand inserted in the daggerboard well. Many new sailboards have a bit of flashing (ridges left by the mould) on the well bottom that can cause injury.

Wooden daggerboards warp. They warp in situations where one side dries faster than the other. The best care for a daggerboard is to hang it up when it's not in use so that both sides will dry

equally fast. The worst treatment for a daggerboard is to leave it on grass or wet asphalt in hot sunlight; this will warp both edges upward. The only cure for such a warp is to turn the daggerboard over and leave it there until it's straight again.

Many sailboards built since 1978 have polyurethane daggerboards with steel reinforcing wires inside. These daggerboards are nearly impossible to warp, and they do not abrade at the leading and trailing edges as wooden daggerboards do. However, the polyurethane daggerboards are brittle and can be fractured when dropped on a hard surface or in a collision. Repair polyurethane daggerboards with epoxy glue and polyester auto-body filler.

Lines

Lines will wear out with use – especially the outhaul, which will chafe very quickly if you drag the booms over asphalt. When an outhaul goes, you fall in the water in a very unpleasant way, so check it now and again. Inhauls don't go suddenly like outhauls, but it's wise to

Figure 87: *Dacron lines that fray on the end can be sealed by melting the end with a flame*

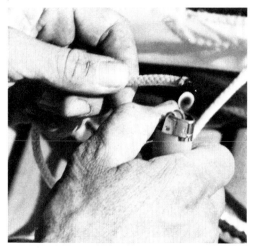

replace them whenever they show a frayed area where the line goes over the 'D' ring.

The sail

Store your sail out of strong sunlight. Strong ultraviolet light will make the fibres brittle, as well as causing the colours to fade. The sail covers available from sailboard dealers are designed both to keep the sail rolled into a compact package and to keep light from harming it.

The most valuable bit of preventive maintenance for your sail, besides storing it out of bright sunlight and *always* slacking the downhaul when the sail is not to be used for several hours, is to make sure that the ends of the battens do not have sharp edges which will abrade and tear the inside of the batten pockets.

Remove and replace battens promptly when they break so the shattered end won't have a chance of wearing through the batten pocket. When sailing for fun and not in competition, battens are not necessary and can be left out. If the sail is an old one and the leech flogs (flips

back and forth) when the battens are removed, completely unbreakable semi-flexible battens can be used during recreational sailing if breakage is a problem.

Dragging your sail around carelessly will wear through the mast sock at the top. If the sock fails while you are sailing, the sail slowly sags down the mast like a pair of wet pyjamas. An emergency in-the-water-fix-it is to tie off the sock above the mast with your downhaul and sail back in without a downhaul.

Fixing a sail sock isn't hard to do, but it requires a strong sewing machine that usually only shoemakers and sailmakers possess. If your home zigzag machine can sew eight layers of Dacron sailcloth, you can do it yourself. Special, stronger, chisel-point needles are available which definitely help the machine. The sock is sewn to the sail with one row of stiches on one side and two rows on the other. Rip out the stiches on the side with only one row, leaving the other side attached. Once the sock is open, bits of Dacron can be sewn over the holes. If your machine isn't strong enough to handle the many

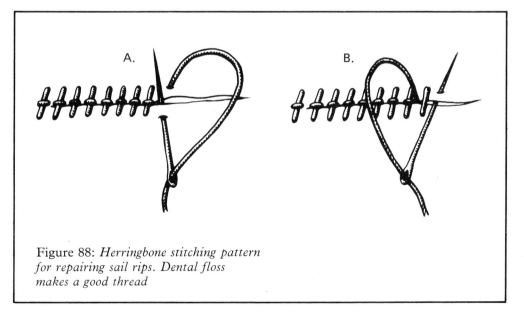

Figure 88: *Herringbone stitching pattern for repairing sail rips. Dental floss makes a good thread*

layers you must sew when you reclose the sock, take the job to a shoemaker or sailmaker.

Sail windows are easy to install with a home zigzag machine. After buying the window material from a sailmaker, cut it to shape and tape it in place using double-sided Scotch tape around the edges. Sew around the outside edge of the window with a zigzag machine; then using a seam ripper, cut out the Dacron about 12 millimetres ($\frac{1}{2}$ inch) inside your first row of stiches. Sew around the cut edge and you are finished. Hawaiians sometimes replace about 20 per cent of their Dacron with windows and have found that this makes their sails *heavier*, so be somewhat conservative with your window additions.

Never sew windows in place with a straight-stitch sewing machine, because the window material will curl slightly away from the sail fabric and project a sharp edge that can cut your knuckles while sailing.

An extensive tear in a sail should be repaired by having the whole panel replaced by a sailmaker. Small rips can be fixed by sewing a hemmed patch over the tear, which should itself be hemmed. A zigzag machine will do the best job. If a sail rips when you are far from Dacron thread and handy sailmakers, waxed dental floss makes a good substitute thread. The best hand stitching pattern is shown in Figure 88.

The U-joint

Universal joints rarely give trouble but, if you have an old one with bolts holding it together, you should remove the nylon nuts and replace them with stainless-steel acorn nuts to prevent scratching yourself on the bolt ends. The vertical bolt often comes loose, so put two steel (not necessarily stainless) $\frac{3}{8}$ inch nuts back-to-back in replacement of the $\frac{3}{8}$ inch nylon nut and the unit will last indefinitely.

Buying a used system

If you are purchasing a used sailboard, your judgement of value should rest on consideration of these things:

1 *Shape of sail*: Does the leech flutter when it is rigged and properly trimmed? A fluttering leech is annoying and indicates that the sail is 'blown out' and will not be very fast.
2 *Condition of the top surface of the hull*: Soft areas where the rider stands develop from much use in waves from the rider bouncing up and down on the deck. A mast-step well that has come loose from the foam inside is a potential problem but, so long as the step well hasn't split and the board is still dry inside in that vicinity, a loose mast-step well is repairable.
3 *Condition of the skeg box*: Just about any damage here is not to be tolerated, as skeg boxes are difficult to repair. You should unscrew and remove the skeg and look for cracks – usually caused by accidents during transportation of the board.
4 *Condition of the mast*: Vertical white cracks in the epoxy show points of incipient failure, especially if they are just above the boom tie point.
5 *Don't be too concerned about*:
(a) Bumps or pits on the bottom of the hull. Many boards have them and they don't impair speed.
(b) Repaired daggerboard wells. If the repair was done correctly there should be no problems. Also, the well is not difficult to repair.

Stopgap measures

There are several jury rigs that a sailor ought to be aware of, to facilitate self-rescue in the event of a hardware failure. In the case of a universal-joint or mast-step failure, the downhaul can be taken off the sail and tied between the remaining U-joint parts and either to the mast 'T' itself or to the daggerboard strap. If a W-spring breaks, the downhaul can be tied around the booms just behind the boom bumpers – this will keep the rig intact while you limp home.

A broken boom presents a real problem. If the wind was strong enough to break a boom, you should probably not attempt to sail hard on the remaining one, since this single boom will now have much greater strain on it and might be broken in the attempt to use it. When a boom goes it's time to roll the sail and paddle.

As a last word, if you are tempted to make a change here and there in the rig – *don't* if you want it to conform to racing regulations. Check with the Windsurfer Class Rules to see if your modification is covered. Adding cleats, for example, is specifically forbidden, as is wrapping the booms with anything to improve grip or stiffness. If you really like to experiment with equipment, the Open Class is for you. You can even build your own board from the ground up!

Chapter Ten
Clothing

Wetsuits

You start by getting a wetsuit. This is the single most important accessory you will own, so its purchase should be carefully considered. The best advice you can get concerning wetsuits (beyond what you can learn from these pages) will come from people who have sailed in your area for a while. But your individual physical needs for warmth should certainly play a part in your decision, too. Some people do get colder – or anyway feel more uncomfortable when they are cold – than others. Also, consider in which seasons you intend to sail. If you like really strong wind, for example, that may put you on the water more often in the winter than the summer, as winter storm-winds are always the most powerful of the whole year.

The most important factor to consider when choosing your wetsuit is not the *water* temperature, but rather the *air* temperature where you sail. Keep in mind that, even if you fall now and then, the time spent dry and sailing is far longer than the time spent in the water. While still remembering your need for warmth, avoid getting a wetsuit that is inappropriately thick or one that covers too much skin surface. Wetsuits can be very hot. For air temperatures down to about 13°C (55°F), a 3 or 5 millimetre ($\frac{1}{8}$ or $\frac{3}{16}$ inch) thick shoulders-to-ankles 'long john' is, I believe, the appropriate item. In places that average 8°C (15°F)

Figure 89 (opposite)

warmer, a shoulders-to-knees 'short john' will suffice. Never get a suit that has arms connected to the body. Buy a separate jacket if you feel you need covering for your arms, which will generally be true for sailing in 10°C (50°F) conditions. The only time that the traditional 7 millimetre ($\frac{1}{4}$ inch) thick diving suit, with its separate pants and jacket, should be used is when it is really cold, 4°C (40°F) or thereabouts.

A wetsuit jacket used for windsurfing should be a 3 or 5 millimetre thick neoprene model with short sleeves, the sleeves stopping just above the elbow.

Figure 90: *The 3 millimetre ($\frac{1}{8}$ inch) thick long-john wetsuit is the most useful type a windsurfer can own*

Because you bend your arms often while windsurfing, long sleeves will reduce your capacity for endurance by about 50 per cent for, with each movement of your arm, you must compress the suit neoprene at the inside of the elbow. You lose considerably more endurance capacity if the suit jacket is 7 millimetres thick. Many people make a windsurfing jacket out of an old diving jacket by snipping off the jacket arms. (To protect your toes against occasional nicks from the stainless-steel hardware on your sailboard, you can make a universal-joint cover for summertime barefoot sailing out of one of the clipped-off arms.)

Your suit should fit snugly. Since a 3 millimetre thick suit is an exceptionally stretchy garment, the inexpensive mass-produced models will fit nearly everybody. This is not true with all 5 or 7 millimetre thick models. If your body size is not standard, you may have to have any 7 millimetre ($\frac{1}{4}$ inch) suit pieces that you want made to measure.

Some people go windsurfing in cotton T-shirts. It's not a bad idea if what you need is sunburn protection; but, if you are after some warmth, a T-shirt won't work unless the shirt stays dry. When the shirt gets wet, the water evaporating from it will make it far colder than bare skin. If you want to wear a shirt in your quest for warmth, a better idea is a spinnaker jacket in the form of a loose, unlined snap-front windbreaker. This garment is lightweight, offers no resistance to arm movement, and will keep the spray away from your body. Spinnaker jackets pick up little water and dry very quickly. Remarkably enough, a spinnaker jacket will be nearly as warm as a wetsuit jacket, because water on your skin underneath the windbreaker will not evaporate quickly and carry away body heat.

Footwear

Most wetsuit boots cannot be used for windsurfing, as they tend to roll around your foot and roll you off the board. These problems don't become apparent unless the wind is over force 3, but they can be a serious annoyance. The best way to add traction and provide protection and warmth for your feet is to wear windsurfing boots, designed specifically to assist in gripping the surface of your board. There are many differing brands on the market, at varying prices; a good dealer will advise you about the best for your particular needs.

A lot of people think windsurfing in shoes is infra dig. If traction is all that you want, you can always rough up your board with a coarse-grit power sander and keep sailing barefoot. There are reasons besides traction, however, that argue for wearing shoes. I became a convert to shoes after several accidents involving shoreside rubbish. Only after I decided to wear shoes for protection did I find out that with shoes I slipped less in strong winds. For one whole season I was nearly unbeatable in any high-wind race – just because I'd be the only one sailing in boots.

Figure 91: *Special shoes for windsurfing, such as these made by Adidas, are ideal*

Beaches and shoes don't go well together, especially when you don't wear socks and the sand in the shoes chafes against your feet. Still, even in areas with warm water, it's a good idea to wear shoes most of the time. Many places have coral, like Tahiti. Wearing shoes there, I was able to sail out to the reef on my sailboard and then hop off onto the coral to go exploring. In other places there's the problem of sea urchins. One of my San Francisco friends stepped on one and got a shoe full of spines. I saw a German who did it barefoot; not pleasant.

Accessories

People who wear glasses have special problems whenever they engage in water sports. The best thing is not to wear them while windsurfing but, if your vision is no better than 20/50, you may have to wear them. A lot of the enjoyment of windsurfing is lost when you miss seeing waves and crash on them, or mistake your team-mates for opponents in Buoyball. It's best to wear an old pair with curving spring earpieces that wrap securely behind the ears, with an elastic band or safety string attached, too. The glasses should be coated with anti-fog compound when you sail in salt water. Wearing contact lenses is a potentially expensive risk.

Especially if you are sailing in cold water, take off any rings before going out, or you may lose them. Cold fingers are smaller and wet fingers are slippery, and a valuable ring can easily slide off.

If your hands get really cold, buy a pair of water skiers' gloves. They are made of a thin, rubberized cloth which won't tire your hands, and they'll slightly improve your grip. Don't use diver's neoprene gloves; constantly bending their thick material will tire your hands very rapidly. If your hands get *sore*, try some gymnasts' hand grips. They much reduce the problem of palm blisters.

For timing my starts when racing, I use a true Scuba diver's wristwatch, which has a crown that screws down and seals the setting mechanism. This watch is very waterproof and yet is much less expensive than the yachting watches, which *do* have the advantage of push-button timing sequences.

Chapter Eleven
Transport

Although cars come in many sizes and shapes, most will adapt to carting windsurfing sailboards. Roof racks are available to fit nearly all hardtop cars, and almost any of these racks can be used to carry one sailboard. I found out very early, though, that it is a good idea to get a first-class rack. My first roof rack blew off my car in a crosswind while I was driving at moderate speed (72 kilometres or 45 miles per hour). My boat went with it. The polyethylene board came through with only a few scratches, but the sail couldn't be used until the torn clew was repaired. And, of course, for the rest of that trip I was really worried about that rack. Better to have a rack and tie-down system that inspires confidence.

The best roof racks are those which attach to the rain gutters on the sides of the roof with mechanical clamps. Racks of this type are often simply two independently mounted bars with no connection provided between the front and rear bars. These bars should not be placed closer than $\frac{3}{4}$ metre apart or further than $1\frac{1}{2}$ metre apart. Spacing that's too close will not give adequate support during turns, while spacing that's too wide will tend to change the shape of the board, allowing the middle to sag.

If the car's rain gutter slopes downwards at a large angle at the point where the rear rack bar attaches, a length of wire or cable or a solid bar connection should be made between the front and rear rack bars. This will keep the back one from tipping over or sliding down the gutter.

The weakest point of any rain-gutter rack, the point where my first rack failed, seems to be the clip of metal that goes under the edge of the rain gutter. The clip is always made of thin metal, since the car door would brush it in opening if the metal were too thick; the only thing that may vary is the width and quality of the clip. Only purchase a rack on which the clips are at least 5 centimetres (2 inches) wide. These clips should be checked periodically when they are in use to make sure they are not losing their bend around the edge of the gutter.

There are a number of roof racks on the market with bars that rest on pads or cups on the roof of the car itself. If the pads are located very far in from the edge of the roof, carrying even one sailboard may dent the car's top. You may have to buy this type of rack, however, if your car does not have rain gutters. It is held on with webbing that clips into the window channels. Don't trust this webbing alone for the security of your board. It is wise to tie additional ropes from the sailboard to other fixtures on the car, as well as to the rack.

Some racks come with rubber 'bungie' cords to be used as tie-down lines. These rubber ropes should never be used without a safety line tied across with the front bungie. Many sailboards have been blown off a car top when held down with bungies alone, because no matter how hard a bungie is pulled when being attached it can always stretch some more.

For a very quick and secure tie-down, use web straps made with a tension spring in the centre and a take-up loop at one side. These straps come with some surfboard racks, and can sometimes be

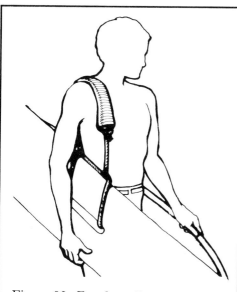
Figure 92: *For short distances a simple carry-strap helps ease the load*

purchased separately from a dealer. They are great items for their qualities of strength and safety, but the flat straps will occasionally vibrate or 'sing' in the wind caused by the car's motion. If this annoys you, put a twist or two in the strap.

When carrying more than one sail-board on a two-bar roof rack, the usual practice is to place the boards upside down, skegs forward, on top of each other, stacked with the lowest one far enough forward that the tail of the one above it comes to the skeg, and the next one up similarly stepped back. The sails

are piled atop the boards. Care should be taken to place the mast steps inside the line of the car's bumper so that passers by will not cut their faces on the universal joint. Since the mast tip is soft and blunt, there is little danger of injury to anyone if this end sticks out, but place a white flag at each end.

When two or three sailboards are carried on top of one another on a rack that has round bars or small square bars, the rack must be padded to prevent the formation of permanent dents in the surface of the board in contact with the rack. Some people replace round bars with lengths of two-by-fours to prevent denting their boards.

Owners who are fearful of theft should build custom racks with lock-down bars that extend across both sail and board, much the same way that a ski rack is constructed. You can set up another security system by running a bicycle chain through the daggerboard well and locking that onto the rack or round the doorframe on the car. Insurance to cover your sailboard against losses due to theft or accident is easily obtained from sailboard dealers.

Boards can be carried on convertibles if a support is provided from the back bumper, similar to a bicycle carrier, while the front of the board is supported on the top of the windscreen frame. If a support is built up from the windscreen frame, and it is made high enough, the soft top can be raised and lowered without removing the board.

Chapter Twelve
Special Equipment

For racing, windsurfing sailboards must conform to a standard design. Someone who enters a regatta with equipment modified from the way it left the factory risks disqualification. The one-design rule is intended to prevent windsurfing races being dominated by wealthy competitors who can afford every expensive innovation – as happens in so many sailing-boat classes. I am in favour of strict interpretation of this rule.

The rule, however, really cramps the style of people like me who just love to tinker with hardware. When I race, I race totally stock equipment, but there are lots of nifty gadgets that I have heard about, poked my fingers into, and tried, that can make a sailboard faster, more manoeuvrable, or more convenient. Many, many pages would be required to catalogue the alterations that have already been tried. I will list here only what I consider to be the best modifications or additions to the stock sailboard, and I will try to describe just a few of the wild and woolly creations that some really radical tinkerers have developed in the search for the ultimate free-sail machine.

Daggerboards

The plank that ends up being a daggerboard is more subject to modification than any other part of the boat – and with good reason. Small changes in daggerboard construction make more difference in sailboard performance than do changes of similar complexity to any other part. Basically, in high winds, while travelling at high speeds, it is not necessary to have as much daggerboard side-profile area as is provided with the stock design. Also, people who are just 'playing' on their boards – and not trying to get somewhere (as in a race) – tend to go back and forth on reaching courses; they don't attempt much upwind sailing, so they don't need a full-size daggerboard either. For either high-wind sailing or for play, it's good to have the daggerboard area a bit further back, placing the centre of lateral resistance further astern, so that the boat heads off the wind faster and has more directional tracking ability going downwind. Thus the usual 'play' daggerboard is smaller and rakes aft faster at a steeper angle. The 'Hawaii' daggerboard is like this, and it also has a ramp-like shape where it goes into the daggerboard well. It also has no cap on top. This capless, ramp design allows you to pile your daggerboard into a coral head at 20 knots and ensure the back of your daggerboard well survives the experience. The daggerboard will simply bounce out through the bottom of the board.

In very high winds, a daggerboard is totally unnecessary when going downwind or on reaches, yet many people are annoyed by the spouting water that shoots up out of the daggerboard well when it is left unfilled. A small lightweight plug can be made to fill the well when you are on downwind courses; many well-equipped sailors carry these too as part of their 'quiver' of special equipment.

People who enjoy reaching, yet want to go upwind a bit more proficiently than the little 'Hawaii' daggerboard allows, have designed a daggerboard that twists around underneath the board and heads straight aft towards the skeg. This daggerboard has roughly the same area as the standard model. It tends to slow the turning rate significantly, however, since the daggerboard is aligned in the direction of travel. The popular name for this daggerboard is 'the monster' because it looks misshapen.

A more sophisticated piece of equipment is the swinging or 'Charchulla' daggerboard, which can be placed in a near-vertical position for upwind sailing and an aft-raking position for downwind sailing.

Skegs

The skeg is another part of the system that sees a lot of changes. The effect of wind speed on boards with modified skegs is roughly opposite to the effect on boards with modified daggerboards. Small skegs work fine in light winds; bigger ones are needed to maintain tracking stability in stronger winds. In a wind less than force 3, you can take the skeg completely off and sail your board quite well, with marvellously fast tacking agility. It is nearly impossible to sail a skegless sailboard, however, if the wind is much over force 3. The darned thing will fishtail like a frightened shark.

The uphaul

Many people become annoyed at having to swing the mast parallel to the board to retrieve the uphaul; so they tie a length of small line or shock cord to the middle of the uphaul and to the mast base, forming a loop, in order to keep the uphaul within easy reach. Racing rules allow modification since it is categorized as a lengthening of a line, which is always permitted. I don't like to sail boards that have been modified in this manner, though, since I usually step through the loop while tacking and fall

flat on my face. This change also effectively shortens the uphaul, making rope gybes with a wide-flung sail impossible. Once again, however, the Hawaiians have come up with a solution that is really clever. They take a 3 metre (10 foot) length of the standard open-weave polypropylene line used for the uphaul, and carefully feed a 3 millimetre ($\frac{1}{8}$ inch) piece of rubber bungie cord through the centre of the uphaul down its entire length. They attach it to the booms with the usual knot (or sometimes a snap shackle), and then stretch the bungie to leave only about $1\frac{1}{4}$ metre (4 foot) unstretched length inside the uphaul. The free end is then knotted and tied with a small line to the downhaul strap. The springy cord inside the uphaul will contract the 3 metre line into a $1\frac{1}{2}$ metre line and leave it tight against the mast where it will not be in the way. Yet, while pulling up the mast or while gybing, the whole 3 metre length can come into play.

Sails

There are several special sails available. Two common models are the 'high-wind' sail (3.99 square metres/43 square feet) and the 'mini' sail (2.79 square metres/30 square feet). Both of these sails have socks which go the full height of a standard mast, but the sail itself does not go the entire distance up the sock. Either of these sails can be quickly interchanged with the standard sail since they are designed to use the same mast and booms. Both sails are made without battens but each has a window.

The mini sail is useful for teaching beginners in winds over force 2 and for use by children who weigh less than 35 kilograms (80 pounds). This sail does not extend all the way to the boom ends; thus, when using it, an extension line must be tied to the outhaul so that the line will reach all the way to the outhaul cleat. If the line is not extended, the

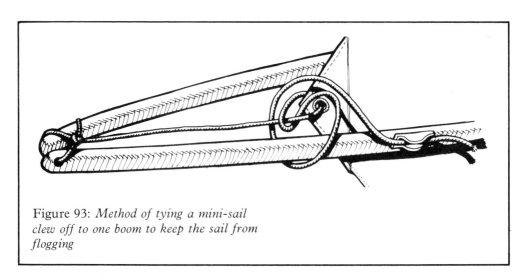

Figure 93: *Method of tying a mini-sail clew off to one boom to keep the sail from flogging*

outhaul must be tied directly onto the clew. It is good practice to tie the outhaul off to a boom on one side to keep the end of the sail from flogging (Figure 93).

The high-wind sail is a superb creation. Every sailboard owner should have one. In winds up to force 5 it is fairly ineffective, true – but, in winds over that, it propels a sailboard like a missile. I have personally sailed a board equipped with a high-wind sail around a triangular course with 200 metre legs in a wind that was a *measured* force 7 to 9 (35 to 50 m.p.h.). The sailboard went so fast it started skipping like a stone. The centre of pressure on this little sail is very low, so it gives a powerful *driving* sensation when you have the right wind for it. Almost every high-wind addict agrees that the greatest windsurfing excitement comes with using this sail in a force 5 or stronger wind.

A sail with a size of 4.55 square metres (49 square feet) is popular among sailors who live in areas where the winds stay between force 4 and force 5 for long periods of time, as they do in the Hawaiian islands. This sail, sometimes called the 'all-round' sail or 'marginal' sail, is usually cut with a concave leech so that it does not need battens. It is so

close to the size of a standard size sail that it can serve as a 'play' sail to keep from wearing out an owner's racing sail.

The original 5.2 square metre (56 square foot) Windsurfer sail was designed for winds averaging force 3. Sailboarders who live in localities where the wind is usually less than that average have built larger sails for their craft. This is easily accomplished without changing the spar set significantly by making a longer dowel for the mast base, in order to hold the mast tube higher off the board. 'Big Rig' sails of 8.36 square metres (90 square feet) are currently in production. Those who have sailed a 'big rig' say that they significantly add to one's stability in wavy regions where the wind is light. In fact they make it almost impossible to fall. It is something like having a parachute. If you sheet in while falling to windward in even a very light breeze, the big sail will just slowly and softly loft you back up. Incidentally, the standard sails used on Ostermann Windgliders (see page 75) are bigger than those used on Windsurfers: 5.8 square metres for the Windglider as opposed to 5.2 square metres for the Windsurfer. The Windglider factory also has a standard production sail available for its product that boasts an area of 7.9 square metres. These larger sizes are useable in southern Germany where the winds are notoriously weak.

Another go-fast arrangement for a windsurfing sail is the use of full-length battens, such as those on many catamaran sails This certainly does work to make the sail faster upwind, since the full-length battens help create a more nearly perfect aerofoil out of the sailcloth. You pay for your speed with additional weight in the rig, which makes it harder to lift the sail from the water.

Quite a few designs have been tried for reefing windsurfing sails. In one method, part of the front area of the sail is fastened to the mast with multiple small ties down the entire vertical distance. By another method, an extension is sewn onto the sock tip, allowing the sail to drop down the mast, with the excess sailcloth at the bottom held out of the way with Velcro tape. A third method simply zips off a large piece of the leech edge of the sail. All the techniques enable the sailor to reduce the standard sail to a reefed size that is close to that of the high-wind sail.

The harness

Some people like to be out on the water enjoying their sailboards for a long time at one spell. Other people like to race them against large sailing boats rather than against other boards. Both of these groups have come up with what is essentially a windsurfing trapeze harness, which allows you to hook up for an easier, even a one-handed, ride. Windsurfing trapeze harnesses have been around at least since 1973, when the Charchulla brothers of Germany first developed a workable system. The best trapeze-harness arrangement to date is the one developed jointly by a number of Hawaiian sailboarders, and independently by David Grasspaugh in Oklahoma. The sailor wears a chest-high harness with a hook facing downwards in the middle (some harness hooks can be used facing upwards). On each boom, a cord about 1 metre long is tied to two bands of webbing which go around the boom – one fore, one aft (sometimes just a knot is used at front, instead of a band) – so that the cord lies parallel to the boom in the area which is usually closest to one's chest while sailing. When going upwind, the sailor 'hooks in' by lifting the boom and engaging the line under the hook, keeping the line tightly stretched along the boom by leaving the bands far apart. When downwind, the bands are brought closer together which allows the boom to move further away from the sailboarder's body.

Sailing with a 'Hawaii harness' is tricky and should be attempted only by expert sailboarders. Failure to unhook quickly when a mistake is made with the sail leads to a violent fall that can break a boom or mast. Even expert harness sailors sometimes wrap extra fibreglass around their masts a foot up and down from the boom line to strengthen them.

If you plan to use a harness, you should very carefully adjust the opening

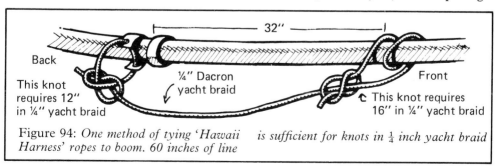

Figure 94: *One method of tying 'Hawaii Harness' ropes to boom. 60 inches of line is sufficient for knots in $\frac{1}{4}$ inch yacht braid*

Figure 95: *With a harness, one-handed or even no-handed sailing is possible*

of the hook to allow for proper ease of disengagement. The hook can be bent open further with a screwdriver to allow more easy disengagement, or it can be crushed together in a vice to reduce accidental disengagement.

The harness has one great advantage that has stimulated the rapid spread of its use throughout the windsurfing community: it makes upwind sailing nearly effortless. Using a harness, you can sail upwind on the same tack for hours! Unfortunately, this effortless windward ability can sometimes lure an incautious sailboarder to upwind points from which it can be difficult to return; it is both hard and hazardous to use a harness when sailing dead downwind, as under these conditions a fall into the sail – common among harness users – will also be a fall directly onto the nose of the board. When sailing with a 'hook', you will probably have to disengage the harness in order to sail the downwind legs, and your remaining arm strength must be adequate to go the downwind

distance. Sliding the back web strap all the way forward to the front knot is a good practice while running (and not using the harness), as this minimizes the opportunities for the hook to engage the line accidentally.

Variations in design

Variations on the original Windsurfer design are of interest since they represent a multitude of experiments with small design features. A survey of the most popular craft built by competing companies shows that the successful variations are not strikingly different from the standard Windsurfer. This is because the Windsurfer was designed for good performance in a wide variety of sailing situations and thus was built as a compromise among the various possible designs. Manufacturers who build for the general market usually make the same compromises. However, if a designer seeks to maximize performance in a particular sailing situation, it is certainly possible to do so by going to one or another extreme.

Good upwind performance is usually the deciding factor in racing. To achieve that, free-sail systems that are built to be fast in average racing conditions – light wind and flat water – are usually built with taller masts and more sail area. Specialized racing hulls are also usually made longer, narrower, and with a V-shaped bottom.

When most people go out for a day of recreational sailing, however, they rarely spend their time going upwind. Instead, they sail mostly on reaches. A flat-bottomed, relatively wide but short board is easier to sail on a reach, especially if it has more than one skeg at the tail. Contrast this with the best racing hull designs, especially those with V bottoms like the Porsche Sailboard and the HiFly. These boards are very difficult to sail on broad reaches and runs as their V hulls

Figure 96: *The Hi-Fly features a boat-type V-bottom which greatly improves upwind performance*

tend to veer off to one side or another when encountering a wave from behind. Also, since these and other strictly 'racing' boards are longer than a standard Windsurfer, they tend to turn less quickly. That means it is harder to perform certain freestyle tricks on them.

Boards that are wider, like the TC-36, have been found to roll less. This is a nice feature for beginners, but it detracts somewhat from the sensation you can get from banking through turns when you are more skilful. Sailboards that are longer in volume tend to give less of an advantage to lightweight sailors in races and are also easier for beginners to sail.

Many of the competitor craft have daggerboards that are thicker and more hydrodynamically correct than the one used on the original Windsurfer. On many, the daggerboards swing back to provide a high-wind daggerboard effect when desired. A buyer must make sure that the daggerboard can be completely removed while sailing and can be easily carried, because in a very high wind having *any* daggerboard in the water is going to impair performance.

Many of the copies use a fibreglass board. This, being harder than poly-ethylene, is more likely to bruise the operator in falls, and is also more subject to fracture. Fibreglass is easily repaired but polyethylene needs repair less often. The tools for polyethylene repair (hot-melt glue gun and a torch) are less commonly owned than those used for fibreglass repair (a trowel and an electric sander). Many fibreglass boards have a ridge along the side where the top half was glued to the bottom half. This ridge wears on your stomach when you climb aboard. Further, if it is was not glued properly, the board can split apart. Polyethylene boards are made in one piece. Thus there is no seam on the side, so they cannot break there and are not so likely to abrade your stomach.

The state of the art in free-sail systems has advanced considerably with inno-vations in materials technology. It is now possible, for example, to build masts that weigh the same or less than the standard epoxy-fibreglass model, but which offer two or more times the stiffness. These masts, made of graphite or Kevlar, give high-wind sail performance to craft carrying as much sail as the standard Windsurfer sail, because a more rigid mast means the sail can be made to keep a more correct shape. These materials have also been applied to hull manu-facture, producing boards that weigh up to 30 per cent less than those of fibreglass

Figure 97 (above): *The Windsurfing International Inc. 1976 Windsurfer Star hull design which was used in setting the 1976 free-sail-machine speed record. Note that the 'tunnel-hull' Star is wider and has a shorter daggerboard-to-skeg distance. The Star has a skeg like the standard Windsurfer, though it was not attached when the photo was taken*

Figure 98 (below): *Skate-sailing, which has been practised at least since 1879, has many similarities to windsurfing*

or polyethylene. The cost of such construction is high; hulls and masts so made are presently three to four times more expensive than those made from the more conventional materials.

In Europe, sailboard design is advancing from regatta to regatta. The Open Class caters for all other makes of sailboard that fall within restrictions set out by the IBSA (International Board Sailing Association). This class is producing sailboards that resemble miniature racing dinghies and are very difficult to sail in winds exceeding 15 knots. Their hull shape is curved and acts in a displacement manner, unlike the planing hull of the classic Windsurfer. They are very much faster upwind because of their decreased wetted area in relation to waterline length, and competition between rival 'works' teams is as intense as that in any motor racing Grand Prix, and the financial stakes are becoming almost as high.

Another new class is already well underway in Europe. Multi-sail free-sail craft have been built for the last few years by Fred Ostermann GmbH and by several other manufacturers.
There is now a sizeable fleet of two-sail 'Tandem Windgliders' on the continent. These craft are very fast and require learning a new set of skills, since coordination between the two sailors is an absolute necessity.

Tandem racing is now organized by a group called the International Tandem Association. The association has set some special rules for its events. Sails may be changed after each course, but replacing one of the sailors during a regatta is not permitted. The two people who start on a tandem together must finish together, but it doesn't matter in which positions on the board they remain or how many sails they use to power their craft. In a big wind the crew might decide to mount just one sail and operate it together! Since the big tandems are so fast, the courses for their races are much

Figure 99: *The hydrofoil set-up designed for the standard Windsurfer hull*

longer than for windsurfing regattas – 800 to 1000 metres between marks on occasion. This is such a great distance that it is sometimes difficult to see from one buoy to another. For tandem racers, divers' wristwatch-style compasses are a good accessory. The 1976 Tandem World Championships were won by the only male/female team that entered, Dirk and Bep Thijs of Holland. Both were former European Windsurfing Champions, in men's and women's divisions respectively.

When the Windsurfer's original inventors, Hoyle Schweitzer and Jim Drake, obtained their patents, they received the rights to apply for their free-sail system to machines intended for any type of terrain: ice, snow, and land included. Needless to say, many sailboard owners have tried various adaptations to their sai's.

The most unusual of the landsurfers is the design of Patrick Carn of France. This device has a small platform equipped with four large, soft, balloon tires, which roll easily on flat beach sand. For travel on asphalt surfaces, several other experimenters have found that the stock windsurfing sail rig, less the universal, adapts quite handily for use as a skateboard sail. A bump of rubber or plastic is built up on the nose of the skateboard to fit inside the hollow mast tube, to give the rig some purchase on the skateboard. You have to be both a very good skateboarder and a fair windsurfer to operate one of these systems.

Sailboard sails also adapt quite readily to ice craft. This is logical because systems very similar to the windsurfing free-sail system have been used by ice skaters since 1879. Many people have rigged skates to the bottom of sailboard hulls. In France, both an ice-skating hull and a snow-skiing hull for use with windsurfing sails are in production.

Windsurfing is such a new sport that it is impossible to speculate on what other inventions will pop up in the realm of special hardware. I hope I will have the opportunity to try out every clever person's new idea. After all, curiosity is what led me to try windsurfing in the first place, and I have never regretted that experiment!

Appendix One
Wind Speeds

Beaufort number	Knots	m.p.h.	Metres per second	Appearance of water	Sail size for enjoyable Windsurfing
0	Under 1	Under 1		Water like a mirror	5.2 sq. m.
1	1–3	1–3	5–2	Ripples on water	(56 sq. ft.)
2	4–6	4–7	2–3.5	Small wavelets	standard sail
3	7–10	8–12	3.5–5	Large wavelets, scattered whitecaps	
4	11–16	13–18	5–8	Small waves, many whitecaps	4.55 sq. m.
5	17–21	19–24	8–11	Moderate waves, whitecaps, some spray	(49 sq. ft.) marginal sail
6	22–27	25–31	11–14	Large waves, whitecaps everywhere, spray	
7	28–33	32–38	14–17	Sea heaped up, white foam blown in streaks	3.99 sq. m.
8	34–40	39–46	17–20	Waves of greater length, well-marked white streaks on surface, walking impeded	(43 sq. ft.) high-wind sail
9	41–47	47–54	20–24	High waves, sea rolls, streaks everywhere, reduced visibility from spray, walking difficult	
10	48–55	55–63	24–28	Very high waves with overhanging crests, visibility reduced, damage to buildings, trees blown down	
11 +		Seek shelter			

*1 knot =. 514 m/sec

Appendix Two
Scoring System for Windsurfing Races

In a regatta, competitors with fewer points accumulated by the following system are placed above competitors with more points.

● $\frac{3}{4}$ point is given for first place.

● For each place other than first points equal to the place are given.

● Did Not Finish (DNF) earns points equal to the number of starters in the race. (Starters includes those who retired from that race after violating a rule.)

● Did Not Start (DNS) earns points equal to the number of entries in the regatta.

● Disqualified (DSQ) earns points equal to the number of starters in that race plus 10 per cent. Fractions are raised to the next highest whole number.

● *Tie breaking*: a tie shall be broken in favour of the competitor with the most first places, and, should any such competitors remain tied, the most second places, and so on, if necessary, for such races as count for a score. Should this method fail to resolve the tie, the tie shall stand in the final placings of the regatta.

Appendix Three
Summary of Sailing's Right-of-Way Rules

● Sailcraft with booms to left (starboard tack) has right-of-way over sailcraft with booms to right (port tack). (Starboard tack rule)

● If both craft have booms on the same side, the one most downwind has right-of-way. (Leeward rule)

● An overtaking craft must keep clear of the one being overtaken.

● If an obstruction or shoaling water lies in the path of a craft which is giving right-of-way to another, the obstructed craft may call for 'sea room' to navigate around the obstruction.

Appendix Four
Vector Analysis of Forces on a Sailboard

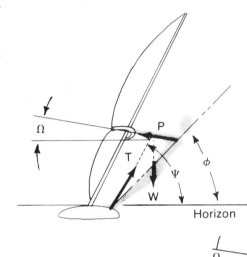

The forces which act on the rider in a plane perpendicular to the direction of travel are:

P = pull felt by the arms
T = thrust felt by the feet
W = sailboarder's weight

At equilibrium:

The sum of the forces in the X direction are $= 0 = P \cdot \cos\Omega - T \cdot \cos\Psi$ **(1)**

The sum of the forces in the Y direction are $= 0 = W - P \cdot \sin\Omega - T \cdot \sin\Psi$ **(2)**

From which we can derive: $P = \dfrac{W}{\sin\Omega + \tan\Psi \cdot \cos\Omega}$ **(3)**

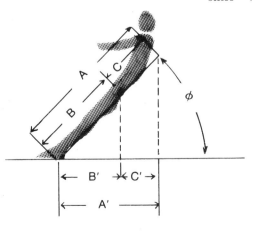

A person's centre of gravity is located at approximately the small of the back. Distance A, from feet to centre of shoulder, and distance B, from feet to small of back, can be measured.

$$A' = A \cos\phi \qquad \textbf{(4)}$$

$$B' = B \cos\phi \qquad \textbf{(5)}$$

$$C' = A' - B' = (A-B) \cdot \cos\phi \qquad \textbf{(6)}$$

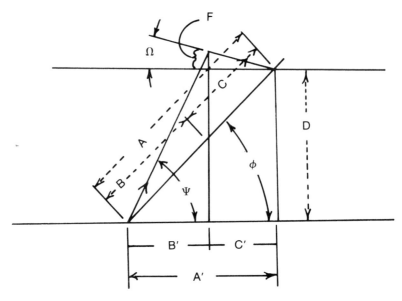

$$F = C' \tan\Omega \qquad (7)$$

$$D = A \sin\phi \qquad (8)$$

$$\text{so: } D + F = A \sin\phi + (A-B) \cos\phi \tan\Omega \qquad (9)$$

$$\text{Now, } \tan\Psi = \frac{D + F}{B'} \qquad (10)$$

Using (5) and (9) in (10) we obtain:

$$\tan\Psi = \frac{A \sin\phi + (A-B) \cdot \cos\phi \cdot \tan\Omega}{B \cos\phi} \qquad (11)$$

$$\tan\Psi = \frac{A}{B} \tan\phi + \frac{(A-B)}{B} \tan\Omega$$

Using (11) in (3) we obtain:

$$P = \frac{W}{\sin\Omega + \cos\Omega \left(\dfrac{A}{B} \tan\phi + \dfrac{(A-B)}{B} \tan\Omega \right)} \qquad (12)$$

Knowing P we can now calculate the forces on the mast and board.

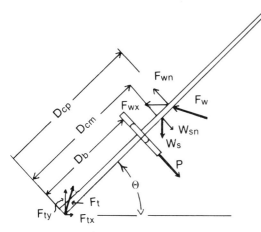

The booms in this diagram have been placed at 90° to the mast. This is the angle that good sailors usually hold them. This means that P will be normal to the mast.

W_s = weight of sail-mast-boom rig

D_{cp} = distance from mast base to the height of the centre of pressure measured along the mast

D_{cm} = distance from mast base to the centre of mass of the rig, measured along the mast

D_b = distance of booms above mast base

F_w = total of aerodynamic lift and drag forces on sail

F_{wn} = portion of aerodynamic forces which acts normal to sail

W_{sn} = weight of rig which is normal to the mast

F_t = total force on mast base

Since the system is momentarily in equilibrium, the sum of the moments around the mast base are 0, which implies:

$$D_b \cdot P + D_{cm} \cdot W_{sn} = D_{cp} \cdot F_{wn} \qquad (13)$$

By trigonometry:

$$W_{sn} = W_s \cdot \cos \Theta$$

So:

$$\left(\frac{D_b}{D_{cp}}\right) \cdot P + \left(\frac{D_{cm}}{D_{cp}}\right) \cdot W_s \cdot \cos \Theta = F_{wn} \qquad (14)$$

The conditions for equilibrium in the x and y directions are:

$$F_{tx} + P \cdot \sin \Theta = F_{wx} \tag{15}$$

$$F_{wy} + F_{ty} - P \cdot \cos \Theta - W_s = 0 \tag{16}$$

F_s = side force on the daggerboard

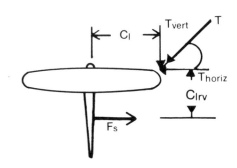

C_{irv} = distance of the centre of lateral resistance below the mast base

T_{vert} = vertical component of the sailboarder's thrust on the board

C_l = distance from the centreline on which the sailboarder is standing

Then:

$$F_{tx} + T_{horiz} = F_s \tag{17}$$

And (taking moments around the mast base)

$$C_l \cdot T_{vert} - F_s \cdot C_{lrv} = 0 \tag{18}$$

So:

$$\left(\frac{C_l}{C_{lrv}}\right) \cdot T_{vert} - T_{horiz} = F_{tx} \tag{19}$$

Now from (1) we obtain:

$$T = \frac{P \cdot \cos \Omega}{\cos \Psi} \tag{20}$$

The vertical component of T is:

$$T_{vert} = T \cdot \sin \Psi = P \cdot \cos \Omega \tan \Psi \tag{21}$$

Replacing tan Ψ with (11) we obtain:

$$T_{vert} = P \cdot \cos \Omega \left(\frac{A}{B} \tan \phi + \frac{(A-B)}{B} \tan \Omega\right) \tag{22}$$

Now $\tan \Psi = \dfrac{T_{VERT}}{T_{HORIZ}}$ So: $T_{horiz} = \dfrac{T_{VERT}}{\tan \Psi} = P \cdot \cos \Omega$ [using (11) and (22)]

Using this last equation with (15), (19) we obtain:

$$P \cdot \left(\cos\Omega \cdot \left(\left(\frac{C_l}{C_{lrv}} \right) \cdot \left(\frac{A}{B} \cdot \tan\phi + \frac{(A-B)}{B} \cdot \tan\Omega \right) - 1 \right) + \sin\Theta \right) = F_{wx} \tag{23}$$

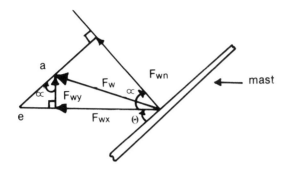

We now solve for F_{wy} in the triangles formed by F_{wn}, F_w and F_{wx}

$$\frac{a}{F_{wn}} = \tan\alpha \therefore a = F_{wn} \cdot \tan\alpha \qquad\qquad (F_{wx} + e)^2 = a^2 + F_{wn}^2$$

$$e \neq F_{wn} \cdot \sqrt{\tan^2\alpha + 1} - F_{wx} \qquad\qquad \frac{e}{F_{wy}} = \tan\alpha \therefore \frac{e}{\tan\alpha} = F_{wx}$$

and using $\alpha = 90° - \Theta$ we get:

$$F_{wy} = \tan\Theta \cdot \left(\frac{F_{wn}}{\sin\Theta} - F_{wx} \right) \tag{24}$$

For the standard Windsurfer: $W_s = 20$ pounds

$C_{lrv} = 14"$, $D_b = 53"$, $D_{cm} = 57"$, $D_{cp} = 78"$

Appendix Five
The Original Windsurfer Sailboard

Overall length: 12 feet (3.6576 metres)

Beam: 26 inches (.6604 metre)

Draught: Daggerboard up – 8 inches (.2032 metre)
Daggerboard down – 24 inches (.6096 metre)

Hull weight: 42 pounds (19.05 kilograms)

All-up weight: 70 pounds (31.75 kilograms)

Sail area: 56 square feet (5.203 square metres)

Hull: Skin is X-link polyethylene. It is filled with urethane foam for stiffness and flotation.

Booms: Teak

Mast: Fibreglass, 15 feet (4.572 metres) with end plug and universal joint. Tube only – 13 feet 8 inches (4.1656 metres)

Flotation: 400 pounds (181 kilograms)

Crew: 1. 2 is possible.

Appendix Six
Speed Records

Fastest speed on a free-sail-system craft in a 20 knot wind:

1975   13.9 knots. 18 foot Tandem Windglider skippered by Clive Colenso at the Player's Speed Trials, England

1976   14.04 knots. 10 foot 10 inch Windsurfer Star hull with a standard Windsurfer sail rig skippered by Matt Schweitzer at the Pacific Multihull Association Speed Trials, USA

1977   19.01 knots. Windglider skippered by Derk Thijs at the Player's Speed Trials, England.

Glossary

Aft: towards the back or tail of the board

Back: (wind) shift to come more from the right

Beam reach: a sailing course at exactly 90° to the wind

Bear off (Head off): turn more downwind

Beat: (verb) sail on a tack upwind; (noun) an upwind course

Blanket: sail upwind of another sailing craft so that its sail lies in the wind shadow of your craft

Broad reach: a course at an angle of more than 90° to the wind but not quite with the wind

Centreboard: serves same purpose as daggerboard (q.v.); rotates around an axle so as to swing down into the water

Close reach: a sailing course between a beam reach and a beat

Come about: turn round so that the wind comes from the other side, with the bow of the board passing through the upwind direction; used while proceeding upwind (cp. GYBE)

Dacron: DuPont registered trademark for its polyester fibre; a very low-stretch material used for sailcloth and lines on the windsurfing free-sail system

Daggerboard: a plank of wood inserted into the hull of a boat or windsurfing sailboard which projects down into the water to reduce sideways slippage. Slides vertically into its 'well' or 'trunk' like a dagger into a sheath

Fast tack: for windsurfers, coming about by pulling on the booms and not touching the uphaul

Gybe: (also **Jibe**): turn round so that the wind comes from the other side, with the tail of the board passing through the upwind direction; used while proceeding downwind (cp. COME ABOUT)

Hard on the wind: proceeding upwind as much as possible; beating

Hawaii harness or **Harness** (also **Trapeze harness**): a device used to aid sailing by attaching the body trunk directly to the booms of a windsurfing free-sail system

Header: a wind shift which turns you away from your chosen destination

Head off: *see* BEAR OFF

Head up (Point up): turn more upwind

Hypothermia: a state of reduced mobility caused by excessive loss of body heat through exposure to cold; can be fatal

Keel: on a large sailing boat, a fixed vertical surface underwater, usually weighted, used to keep the boat from sliding sideways and also to keep the boat upright

Lee shore: the shore that is downwind of your present position

Leeward or **Lee side:** the downwind side of anything

Lift: a wind shift which helps take you towards your chosen destination

Luff: hold the sail so that it is not completely full of wind

Overstand: (said of marks in racing) to sail more upwind of a mark than is necessary to get round it

Pearl: a surfing term used to describe the occasion when the nose of the board dives under a wave and suddenly stops forward movement

Point up: *see* HEAD UP

Port tack: a sailing course when the wind is coming from the left-hand side (or booms to the right if going downwind)

Reach: sail with the wind from the side

Rope gybe: for sailboarders, gybing using the uphaul

Rope tack: for sailboarders, coming about using the uphaul

Run: sail with the wind from astern

Sheet (in): pull in with the back hand so as to fill the sail more completely with wind

Starboard tack: a sailing course when the wind is coming from the right-hand side (or booms to the left if going downwind)

Tack: (verb) in sailing, execute a turn in order to have the wind coming from the other side, either by coming about (q.v.) or by gybing (q.v.). Sailboarders usually mean 'come about' when they say 'tack'

Ugly: a surfboard style. It has a round nose, parallel sides and a square tail; usually made 2.7 to 3.3 metres (9 to 11 feet) long for surfing. Used as the design for the first Windsurfer sailboard

Veer: (wind) shift to come more from the left

Windward: the upwind side of anything.